KU-201-490

How to Pass

SQA NATIONAL 5

Spanish

Kathleen McCormick

Boost

HODDER
GIBSON
AN HACHETTE UK COMPANY

Audio files for the listening tasks in this book are available online. Visit www.hoddergibson.co.uk/audio-how-to-pass-spanish

The Publishers would like to thank the following for permission to reproduce copyright material.

Photo credits

p.2 Halfpoint – stock.adobe.com; **p.3** NIKCOA – stock.adobe.com; **p.5** BRIAN_KINNEY – stock.adobe.com; **p.23** Prostock-studio – stock.adobe.com; **p.26** Alexe – stock.adobe.com; **p.27** Delphotostock – stock.adobe.com; **p.28** Robert Kneschke – stock.adobe.com; **p.29** Sebastiank24 – stock.adobe.com

Acknowledgements

The tables on **pp.vii, 55–57, 61–63, 67** are from the SQA Course Specification for National 5 Modern Languages © Scottish Qualifications Authority.

Every effort has been made to trace all copyright holders, but if any have been inadvertently overlooked, the Publishers will be pleased to make the necessary arrangements at the first opportunity.

Although every effort has been made to ensure that website addresses are correct at time of going to press, Hodder Gibson cannot be held responsible for the content of any website mentioned in this book. It is sometimes possible to find a relocated web page by typing in the address of the home page for a website in the URL window of your browser.

Hachette UK's policy is to use papers that are natural, renewable and recyclable products and made from wood grown in well-managed forests and other controlled sources. The logging and manufacturing processes are expected to conform to the environmental regulations of the country of origin.

Orders: please contact Hachette UK Distribution, Hely Hutchinson Centre, Milton Road, Didcot, Oxfordshire, OX11 7HH. Telephone: +44 (0)1235 827827. Email education@hachette.co.uk Lines are open from 9 a.m. to 5 p.m., Monday to Friday. You can also order through our website: www.hoddereducation.co.uk. If you have queries or questions that aren't about an order, you can contact us at hoddergibson@hodder.co.uk

© Kathleen McCormick 2021

First published in 2021 by
Hodder Gibson, an imprint of Hodder Education
An Hachette UK Company
211 St Vincent Street
Glasgow, G2 5QY

Impression number	5	4	3	2	1
Year	2025	2024	2023	2022	2021

All rights reserved. Apart from any use permitted under UK copyright law, no part of this publication may be reproduced or transmitted in any form or by any means, electronic or mechanical, including photocopying and recording, or held within any information storage and retrieval system, without permission in writing from the publisher or under licence from the Copyright Licensing Agency Limited. Further details of such licences (for reprographic reproduction) may be obtained from the Copyright Licensing Agency Limited, www.cla.co.uk

Cover photo © Olga – stock.adobe.com

Typeset by Aptara, Inc.

Printed in Spain

A catalogue record for this title is available from the British Library.

ISBN: 978 1 3983 1912 7

Contents

What is the course like?

National 5 Spanish will test you on four skills: reading, listening, talking and writing. All of these skills will be taught over the course of your studies by your teacher/lecturer to help you pass the final exam. Three of the skills – reading, listening and writing – will be assessed at the end of the course in an external exam, set and marked by SQA, which will provide you with a grade A, B, C or D. In addition, at some point in the year, you will complete a writing assignment, which will also be marked by SQA, and you will carry out a talking assessment, which will be marked by your teacher.

In this book you will find chapters to help you work on and revise each skill. You will be able to practise responding to reading and listening texts, and useful tips and hints will help you in these areas. In the chapters on talking and writing there is guidance and suggested approaches to help you produce material in both of these skills. The language you will need to know relates to four contexts: **society, learning, employability** and **culture**. On page vii you will find a list of possible topic areas within these contexts that you could expect at National 5.

WWW

- Further information on Spanish National 5 can be found on the SQA website: sqa.org.uk (National 5 Modern languages). Here you will find an overview of the course and the exam in the 'Course Specification' section. You can also find past papers, specimen question papers, transcripts and audio files for listening, and marking instructions.
- Audio files for the listening tasks are available to download here: www.hoddergibson.co.uk/audio-how-to-pass-spanish.

How is my final scaled mark made up?

You will be given a mark for each of the four skills. A potential 120 marks, on which your final grade will be based, are divided up as follows after scaling:

- reading: 30 marks
- listening: 30 marks
- talking: 30 marks
- writing: 30 (15 exam/15 assignment) marks.

This will then be converted into a mark out of 100, making each skill worth 25% of your total.

What do I have to know?

You will need to know basic vocabulary covering a list of topic areas, which you will find in the table on page vii. This will help you listen to and read Spanish more easily, and will also help you produce your own written and spoken Spanish. You will find lists of useful vocabulary with many of the talking and writing preparation tasks, as well as with the listening tasks. Chapter 9 'Vocabulary' will also be useful.

You will need to know the basics of grammar, so that you can write and speak Spanish correctly. This is something you will work on as you go through the course. Some guidelines are at the end of this introduction. You will also find some guidance in Chapter 8 'Opinions and grammatical structures'. There is further work on producing your own Spanish in Chapter 5 'Talking' and Chapters 6 and 7 'Writing'.

You must be able to use a dictionary to help you understand Spanish in the reading exam, and to find words you need for your talking and writing.

What exactly is involved in the exam?

Reading

Reading will be assessed by an external exam. There will be one paper that will include three separate texts, each of up to 200 words. Questions will be set and answered in English. Unusual words may be translated for you in a glossary. You will be allowed to use a Spanish dictionary.

Writing

Writing will be assessed by one piece of work that you will produce after you have done the reading. You will be expected to respond to a stimulus with six bullet points, all of which you must address. The context for the writing is **employability**.

The reading and writing paper will last 1 hour 30 minutes.

You will also write an assignment of 120–200 words under controlled conditions. See Chapter 7 'Writing: the assignment' for details.

Listening

Listening will be assessed by an external exam. There will be two separate parts, one a presentation or monologue, the other a conversation or dialogue. You will hear the Spanish three times, and the whole assessment will last up to 30 minutes.

Questions will be set and answered in English.

You **will not** be allowed to use a Spanish–English dictionary.

Talking

Talking will be assessed by your teacher/lecturer and may be externally moderated by SQA. You will be expected to carry out a spoken presentation and conversation in Spanish. Your presentation must be based on one of the following contexts: **society**, **learning**, **employability** or **culture**. In the conversation, your teacher/lecturer will first ask you questions based on the context of your presentation and will then ask you questions on one of the other three contexts. You will agree both contexts with your teacher. You will also agree with your teacher when your assessment will take place. The presentation will be worth 10 marks and the conversation 20 marks.

Basic grammar

When marking your work, teachers will be looking for accuracy in basic structures. This is straightforward, simple language, and you should be able to show you can do everything listed on pages 20–21.

How do I go about learning vocabulary?

The best way to revise is to practise. Although different people have different ways of learning vocabulary, the following ways might be useful to you.

Hints & tips

✓ Try writing out a list of words, then reading them out. Cover up the Spanish words, and see if you can remember the words in English, and of course the other way round.

✓ Read things over several times on different occasions.

✓ Check your memorising by either covering one part and remembering the other, or by asking someone to do it with you (a friend or parent). If you have someone to help you, ask them to say a word in English, which you have to put into Spanish.

✓ Try to get your words organised into areas, so they all hang together and make sense to you.

✓ Use mind maps of related words.

What kind of vocabulary will I need to know?

On the next page you will find the topic areas that you are likely to be studying as part of your course. You will also find vocabulary lists in Chapter 9 to help you prepare for assessments and to revise.

Contexts, topics and topic development you can expect in National 5 Spanish

Society	Family and friends	Getting on with family members/who have influenced you in your life
		Having arguments
		Ideal parents
		Different types of friends
		Peer pressure
	Lifestyles	Lifestyle-related illnesses
		Advantages and disadvantages of healthy/unhealthy lifestyle
	Media	Impact of TV reality shows
		Advantages/disadvantages of new technology, e.g. internet, mobile phones
	Global languages	Language learning and relevance
	Citizenship	Description of local area as a tourist centre
		Comparison of town and country life
		Being environmentally friendly in the home
Learning	Learning in context	Talk about what learning activities you like/dislike in modern languages/in each subject
		Preparing for exams
	Education	Comparing education systems
		Improving own education system
		Learner responsibilities
Employability	Jobs	Part-time jobs and studying
		Qualities for present/future jobs/future plans
	Work and CVs	Planning, reporting back on work experience
		Reviewing achievements/ambitions
Culture	Planning a trip	Importance of travel and learning a modern language
		Describing your best holiday/trip, attitudes to travel
	Other countries	Aspects of other countries including educational, social, historical, political aspects
	Celebrating a special event	Comparing special occasions/traditions/celebrations/events in another country
		Importance of customs/traditions
	Literature of another country	Literary fiction, e.g. short stories – understanding and analysis
	Film and television	Studying films in the modern language
		Studying television in other countries

How to tackle reading and listening

To help you prepare for the reading and listening parts of the exam, you should be regularly learning and revising vocabulary for the four contexts: **society**, **learning**, **employability** and **culture**. In addition, practice with reading and listening tasks and using a Spanish–English dictionary will help you with time management in the exam.

In both the reading and the listening exams, you will be asked to answer questions in English to show your understanding of the texts. It is important that you practise answering in English to convey this understanding.

Hints & tips

✓ *When you write your answers in English, keep them concise and clear.*
✓ *You don't need to answer in full sentences — just write down the information needed for the answer.*
✓ *Practise answering in English by using the reading and listening examples in this book, as well as SQA past papers and exercises you do in class.*

WWW

For National 5 Spanish exam and specimen papers go to:
www.sqa.org.uk/sqa/47415.html

Reading

In the reading exam you will read three texts in Spanish and answer questions in English after each one. You should look at past SQA exam and specimen papers to see the style of questions that you will be asked.

When you read a text in Spanish, you should look at the questions first to see what information you need to look for. You won't be required to know every word, but you will need to develop the skill of identifying key words and phrases that relate to the questions being asked.

Familiarise yourself with the types of questions used to assess your understanding. Chapter 3 gives you more information about the question types. The more SQA past paper practice you do, the more familiar you will become with the types of questions used in the reading question paper.

You can also use the reading texts and other Spanish material throughout this book to give you ideas for the writing assignment: there may be sections you can use and adapt depending on your topic.

Hints & tips ⭐

✓ *Using a dictionary is a key part of the reading exam paper. You should practise how to use the dictionary correctly.*

✓ *Remember that the parts of verbs won't be in the dictionary — you need to be able to identify the infinitive of the verb in order to look this up in the dictionary. For example, 'voy' is not in the dictionary — you need to know this is the first person singular ('I' part) of the verb 'ir' (to go).*

Below are three texts from three different contexts (**learning**, **society** and **culture**) to help you practise identifying essential information in a text and develop your skills in answering questions.

Learning: Education

You read an article about the IES Los Olmos high school.

¡Una educación sin limites!

IES Los Olmos ofrece una educación sin igual. Es un instituto pequeño, pero la amplia gama de asignaturas va desde música, lengua extranjera y cultura clásica hasta biología, geología, física y química. Además, hay muchísimas oportunidades extraescolares, por ejemplo, los jueves hay un club de boxeo y los viernes hay un club de esgrima. Se puede asistir a talleres de creatividad – teatro y arte. Este año también tendremos un taller de cine en el salón de actos que ahora cuenta con una enorme pantalla de alta definición.

En el recreo, se puede ir a la biblioteca a leer o usar el ordenador para hacer algunas tareas en línea. Tenemos un gimnasio enorme para hacer deporte y a la una, la cantina sirve comida deliciosa a un precio razonable.

Hints & tips ⭐

✓ *Remember not to look up every word you don't know in the dictionary. The more practice you get with reading, the more you will be able to identify parts of words you already know in other words, or even be able to understand words from their similarity with English. For example, in the first reading text on this page you will find the Spanish noun 'la creatividad'. You may already know the adjective 'creativo/a' (creative), so you should be able to work out that 'creatividad' is the noun: creativity.*

✓ *Spanish words ending with '-dad' have the English equivalent of '-ty', e.g. 'nacionalidad' (nationality).*

Hints & tips ⭐

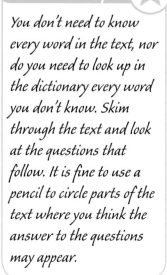

You don't need to know every word in the text, nor do you need to look up in the dictionary every word you don't know. Skim through the text and look at the questions that follow. It is fine to use a pencil to circle parts of the text where you think the answer to the questions may appear.

Questions ❓

1. Name **three** subjects the school 'IES Los Olmos' offers. **3**

   _____

   _____

   _____

2. What extra-curricular activities are available? Complete the sentence. **2**

   On Thursdays there is _____ and on Fridays there

   is _____ .

3. What will the school have this year? **1**

   _____

4. What can you do at break times? State any one activity. **1**

   _____

5. What other details are given about the school? Tick **two** correct boxes. **2**

You can play sport on the sports pitch.	
There is a large gym hall.	
You can't buy food in the school.	
Food is reasonably priced.	

Hints & tips ⭐

If you are asked to tick two correct boxes, only tick two! If you tick three boxes, and two are correct, you will only receive 1 mark for the first correct answer. If you tick all four boxes, you will receive 0 marks!

Society: Media

You read an article about social media and young people.

El aprendizaje digital

Según un estudio reciente, la mayoría de los jóvenes españoles usan frecuentemente las redes sociales para estar conectados con otros, estar al día de lo que ocurre en su mundo y para compararse con otros jóvenes. Se está pasando un poco de moda el uso de ciertas plataformas en línea por su popularidad entre los mayores.

Questions ?

1 According to the recent study, what do young people use social media for? State any **two** purposes. **2**

....

....

2 Why are some online platforms unfashionable with young people? **1**

....

Hints & tips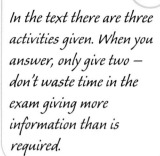

In the text there are three activities given. When you answer, only give two — don't waste time in the exam giving more information than is required.

El estudio señala que los jóvenes en España prefieren las redes sociales que más reflejan su mundo y que contienen lo que les gusta, principalmente el uso creciente de videos o fotos. Cada vez más jóvenes empiezan su conocimiento del mundo digital a una edad temprana: el estudio descubrió que un 68% de los niños de 10 años ya tienen cuentas en muchas redes sociales, aunque el problema es que en algunas hay una edad mínima de uso.

Hints & tips

Remember that you do not need to look up every word in the dictionary. For example, here you might not immediately know 'conocimiento' (knowledge), but you probably do know the verb 'conocer' (to know).

Questions ?

3 What does the study point out about young people's use of social media? State **two** details. **2**

....

....

4 According to the article, what is the problem with younger children having social media accounts? **1**

....

Hints & tips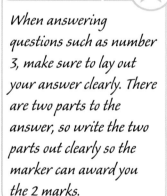

When answering questions such as number 3, make sure to lay out your answer clearly. There are two parts to the answer, so write the two parts out clearly so the marker can award you the 2 marks.

Fernando Hidalgo García, psicólogo de la Universidad de Barcelona, cree que las escuelas tienen la responsabilidad de preparar a los niños para el mundo digital e informarles sobre las redes sociales. "Vivimos en un mundo donde el uso de estas plataformas es cada vez más sofisticado y soy de la opinión de que será fundamental educar a los niños a poder distinguir entre lo que es real y lo que es falso". Además, añade que puede haber mucha manipulación en Internet y que hay que desarrollar las destrezas digitales en los jóvenes de hoy.

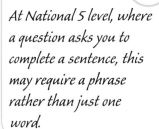

5 a According to Fernando Hidalgo García, what responsibilities do schools have? State **two**. 2

....

....

  b What does he believe needs to happen? Complete the sentence. It will be fundamental to educate children to 1

....

> **Hints & tips** ⭐
>
> *At National 5 level, where a question asks you to complete a sentence, this may require a phrase rather than just one word.*

Culture: Planning a trip

This activity will help you practise selecting relevant and useful information. Although you will not have to do a task like this in the reading exam, the activity will help you develop your skills in reading and selecting the necessary details to answer questions.

Read the blog entry below and then fill in the table that follows to identify the positive and negative aspects of each method of transport mentioned.

> **Hints & tips** ⭐
>
> *Remember you can also use the ideas and structures here to help you prepare for the talking-performance or for the writing assignment.*

¡Hola! En el blog de esta semana voy a hablar de mi experiencia con diferentes medios de transporte. Creo que ya he usado la mayoría de los transportes que existen. Mi favorito es, sin duda, el tren. En mi opinión, los trenes modernos en España son súper rápidos y muy cómodos. Se puede estudiar sin problemas o ver una serie en el móvil.

Sin embargo, me gusta menos viajar en barco porque siempre me mareo. El avión es eficiente y no es tan caro como antes, aunque a veces pierdo tiempo en el aeropuerto con la facturación y las maletas. En la ciudad, es aconsejable moverse en metro debido a la frecuencia de paso de trenes y además ayuda a evitar los atascos. Me enfurece que todavía haya tantos coches y motos en la ciudad; contaminan mucho y son peligrosos.

¡Ah! Adoro la bicicleta. Montar en bici es muy sano, pero cuando llueve o hace mucho frío, es menos atractivo como medio de transporte. Suelo evitar el autobús en mi ciudad porque muchas veces llega tarde y nunca hay asientos disponibles.

Question

Method of transport	Positive	Negative
Train		
Boat		
Plane		
Underground		
Cars and motorbikes		
Bike		
Bus		

Listening

In the listening exam there are two sections. First you will listen to a short monologue (one person speaking), and then you will listen to a conversation in Spanish between two people. Both sections will be based on the same context, which will be the context not covered by the three texts in reading exam. You can read more on this in Chapter 3.

You will answer questions in English for each section to assess your understanding. In the listening exam you will have to:
- read the introduction and questions
- listen to the information
- answer the questions

You will do all of this in a very short space of time, so practice is crucial!

www

Practise time management as much as possible with SQA past papers (**www.sqa.org.uk/sqa/47415.html**). You need to make sure you have time to read, listen, answer, check and make any changes!

You will hear the monologue three times, with an interval of 1 minute between each time. You will then have 2 minutes to read the questions for the conversation. You will then hear the conversation three times, with an interval of 1 minute between each time.

The first time you hear the monologue/conversation, make sure you listen but don't think you have to answer every question at this point. You can note answers in the left margin beside each question – then when you hear the monologue/conversation a second time, check this answer and write it in the space provided. Make sure you score out any notes on your answer page.

Other essential preparation for the Listening exam is learning and revising vocabulary – you cannot use a dictionary in this part of the exam.

It is also good to practise to listen to Spanish as much as possible, both in and outside class. As well as textbook resources, try to listen to Spanish

Hints & tips

There is time built into the exam for you to read the questions — make sure you do this as the questions will signpost what type of information you need to listen out for. There may be key words in a question you need to listen out for. For example, if a question asks about what someone prefers, then you can underline the word 'prefer' in the question and listen out for phrases such as 'lo que me gusta más', 'prefiero' or 'mi...favorito/ preferido es...'.

radio online or watch Spanish programmes to further develop your skills of listening and understanding.

WWW

Listen to Spanish radio and watch Spanish television or reports on:

- www.rtve.es
- www.antena3.com
- www.elpais.com
- www.newsinslowspanish.com
- https://podcast.duolingo.com

In the listening part of the exam, you will not be required to understand every word in Spanish, nor will you be expected to write down every word you hear in an answer. However, using the questions to help guide you to the required information, and regularly revising vocabulary will help prepare you for the tasks.

Chapter 4 gives further details about the type of questions you may come across in the listening exam. Below are three examples of listening tasks. Play and replay these as many times as you need to as this will help you complete the tasks for each listening.

WWW

Audio files for the listening tasks are available to download here: www.hoddergibson.co.uk/audio-how-to-pass-spanish.

Society: Citizenship

🔊 **Monologue.** *Listen to Carlota who compares living in the city with living in a village. She talks about the advantages and disadvantages of both. As you listen, write in English four points she makes about living in a village and four points she makes about living in a city.*

Hints & tips ⭐

In the actual listening exam, remember to score out any notes on your answer booklet and write your final answers clearly in the lined spaces.

Questions ❓

Village	City

Hints & tips ⭐

✓ *Keep your notes concise and in clear English.*
✓ *For this practice exercise, use another sheet of paper for notes and then you can transfer them onto the grid.*

Culture: Other countries

🔊 **Conversation between two people**. *Listen to Serafín and Manuela talking about school trips. Replay the conversation as many times as you need to and note what Manuela says about her trip to Santander.*

Questions ❓

1 When did Manuela go to Santander?   **1**

....

2 How long did she spend there?   **1**

....

3 Where did she stay?   **1**

....

4 What did she do during the day and what did she think of this?   **2**

....

5 What else did she do there?   **1**

....

Hints & tips ⭐

✓ The first two answers are combined in the sentence beginning 'El mes...' so you may have to listen carefully to capture both pieces of information.

✓ Watch out when translating verbs such as 'gustar' (used to indicate when someone likes or dislikes something) and 'encantar' (used to indicate when someone loves something). You need to make sure your answer is accurate to get the marks.

Employability: Jobs

 Monologue. *Listen to four people talking about their future plans.*

Question ❓

For each person, note what they would like to do in the future and try to listen out for any supporting detail such as why they would like to do that job/career and what their skills or interests are.

Marilia: ....

....

Miguel: ....

....

Natalia: ....

....

Carlos: ....

....

Hints & tips ⭐

In this practice exercise you will hear the speakers use different ways of saying what they would like to do. Phrases such as 'mi sueño es' (my dream is...), 'quiero...' (I want...) and 'me gustaría...' (I would like) are all good ways to say what you would like to do. You could use these in your talking and writing preparation too.

Answers and transcripts for reading and listening tasks

Reading answers

Learning: Education

1 Any three from: music, foreign languages, classical studies, biology, geology, physics, chemistry.
2 boxing club; fencing club
3 a cinema workshop
4 go to the library to read/use the computer
5 There is a large gym hall; Food is reasonably priced.

Society: Media

1 Any two from: be connected to others; be up to date with what is going on in their world; compare themselves with others.
2 They are popular with older people.
3 They prefer social media which reflects their world and contains what they like.
4 in some there is a minimum age
5 a better prepare children for the digital world; inform them about the world of social media
  b be able to distinguish between what is real and false

Culture: Planning a trip

Method of transport	Positive	Negative
Train	Very fast and comfortable; can study without any problem on a train or watch a series on your mobile	
Boat		Gets sea-sick
Plane	Efficient; not as expensive as before;	Wastes time with check-in and luggage
Underground	Frequency of trains; helps avoid traffic jams	
Cars and motorbikes		Cause lots of pollution and are dangerous
Bike	healthy	When it rains or it's cold it's not as attractive
Bus		Arrives late; never any available seats

Listening transcripts and answers

Society: Citizenship

Transcript

Ahora vivo en una ciudad cerca de la playa, pero también he vivido en un pueblo cerca de las montañas del norte. Los dos sitios ofrecen cosas buenas y malas; no puedo decidir cuál es mejor.

Vivir en contacto con la naturaleza cerca del pueblo es muy bonito y agradable. Se puede respirar aire limpio y montar en bici sin problemas de tráfico. Yo he montado en bici muchas veces en la ciudad, pero no lo recomendaría. Es peligroso porque hay muchos coches rápidos en la calle. En un pueblo en el campo se puede explorar la naturaleza y visitar granjas con muchos animales como caballos y vacas. En la ciudad hay más ruido y se respira aire más sucio.

[*PAUSA*]

Por otro lado, la ciudad ofrece otras posibilidades. Se puede ir a museos, exposiciones de pintura y obras de teatro. Además, hay más tiendas. En el pueblo es recomendable hacer la compra por Internet. Yo he hecho la compra por Internet muchas veces, pero creo que es mejor ir a las tiendas.

Lo malo de la ciudad es que las distancias son largas y es complicado visitar a amigos que viven al otro lado de la ciudad porque necesitas usar el metro, el taxi o los autobuses públicos. En un pueblo todo es menos complicado y los amigos están cerca. El pueblo también es más barato que la ciudad.

Actualmente me gusta el estilo de vida en la ciudad. ¡Hay tanto que hacer! Hoy me he duchado rápidamente y he desayunado pronto para ir a un concierto al aire libre en un parque en las afueras.

Answers

Any four points for village and for city from the following:

Village	City
Living in contact with nature	Dangerous to cycle as many fast cars
Breathe fresh air	Noisier
Cycle without traffic problems	Dirtier air
Explore nature	Can go to museums, paint exhibitions, plays in the theatre
Visit farms with many animals	More shops
Things less complicated	Long distances so difficult to visit friends
Friends live near	Need to use public transport
Cheaper than the city	Lots to do

Culture: Other countries

Transcript

Serafín: Hola Manuela, yo participo mucho de los viajes de mi instituto. ¿Y tú?

Manuela: Yo también, pero prefiero los viajes largos a las excursiones de un día. El mes pasado estuve una semana en Santander, de intercambio. El viaje me lo pagó mi madre.

Serafín: ¿Qué tal fue?

Manuela: ¡Genial! Me alojé en una casa con mi amiga Elena, con quien siempre me escribo mensajes y correos electrónicos. Estamos en contacto gracias al instituto y a un programa de intercambio con mi insti y el insti de Elena.

Serafín: ¿Y qué hiciste allí?

Manuela: Pues, conocí a la hermana pequeña de Elena, Gabriela, que tiene 9 años y es muy graciosa. Durante el día fui a clases con Elena. Fue un poco difícil, pero me encantó la experiencia. También visité los monumentos de la ciudad y comí mucha comida muy rica porque el padre de Elena es muy buen cocinero. Serafín, ¿nunca has ido de intercambio?

Serafín: No. Realmente me da un poco de miedo estar fuera de mi casa tanto tiempo. Pero mi instituto organiza muchos viajes culturales. Este año ya he visitado Toledo, Valladolid y Zaragoza y pasé dos días en un camping con actividades deportivas.

Answers

1 last month
2 1 week
3 at her friend's/Elena's house
4 She went to lessons with Elena. It was a little difficult but she loved the experience.
5 She visited the city sites and ate delicious food.

Employability: Jobs

Marilia: Soy Marilia. A mi me gustaría ser pintora o vivir del arte en general. Trabajo muy bien en equipo y soy muy creativa. Creo que sería una lástima trabajar en una oficina todo el día. Quiero pintar cuadros, hacer esculturas o decorar casas.

Miguel: Me llamo Miguel. Preferiría ir a la universidad y continuar con mi formación educativa. Creo que es muy importante. Quiero estudiar medicina y hacer la especialidad en cirugía. Mi sueño es trabajar en un hospital y ayudar a los enfermos.

Natalia: Mi nombre es Natalia. Soy bastante práctica y me gustan los coches. Me gustaría ser mecánica. Aún así, me encantaría continuar con mis estudios un poco más y completar mis estudios de idiomas.

Carlos: Soy Carlos. Mi pasión son las matemáticas y los números. Quiero trabajar como mi padre, y ser contable. Tengo buena memoria y muy buenas notas en matemáticas. Además, es un trabajo que paga muy bien.

Answers

For each person there is information about what they would like to do in the future as well as detail on why they would like that career and/or what their skills and interests are.

Marilia
- would like to be a painter or do something with art
- is a team worker and is creative
- wants to paint pictures, do sculptures, decorate houses

Miguel
- would like to go to university
- wants to study medicine and specialise in surgery
- wants to work in a hospital and help sick people

Natalia
- wants to be a mechanic
- is practical and likes cars
- would like to continue her studies more and finish her language studies

Carlos
- wants to be an accountant (like his dad)
- likes maths and numbers
- has a good memory
- gets good marks in maths

Chapter 2

How to tackle talking and writing

Talking and writing are called the 'productive' skills: these are the skills that enable you to produce rather than receive language (reading and listening skills). Throughout the National 5 Spanish course, you will have opportunities to develop talking and writing skills in class – remember it is crucial to also practise them at home.

Talking and writing skills complement each other in terms of development and assessment. For example, as you prepare written material for your assignment and your response to a job advert (in Question paper 1), you will create material that can be adapted for your talking performance – and vice versa. In addition, as you develop your knowledge of grammar, you will also develop greater accuracy in your talking and writing skills.

Talking

Learning vocabulary, revising grammar and practising pronunciation are all key aspects of developing the skill of talking in Spanish.

Arranging vocabulary and sentences you have learned under the broad context headings can help you organise material you can use and adapt to prepare for the talking exam.

Other opportunities to practise talking might include:
- preparing and delivering a short presentation
- responding to and asking questions in a conversation on a set topic
- pair and group work in class
- recording yourself and uploading to a virtual classroom

The presentation

The following is an example of a short presentation on the topic of Lifestyles (in the context of Society). It is organised into three paragraphs. Use this structure when developing the content of your presentation and this will help when you have to learn it for the performance. You can also give it a title. Here the title is *Cómo llevo una vida sana*.

First paragraph

The first paragraph should be an introduction to the general theme. In the example below the theme is stress and how to manage it. Notice how there are two opinion phrases given (*para mí* and *creo que*) which help to establish the speaker's thoughts and opinions on the subject. Using opinion phrases, and other phrases such as *tanto... como* (both) and *claro* (of course) will help you to raise the level of this introductory paragraph.

Try also to avoid always using first-person verbs (the 'I' part). A variety of verbs will enhance your text – in this example the third-person plural (the 'they' part) is used to add variety.

> ### Hints & tips
>
> *At home you can practise talking and writing in Spanish by revising your class notes, recording yourself talking in Spanish and listening to yourself. You can even ask someone at home to ask you questions in English based on the topics you are studying – and you answer in Spanish!*

Para mí, las cosas más estresantes son los exámenes y el trabajo escolar. Creo que las dos cosas me causan estrés porque tanto mis profesores como mis padres me ponen mucha presión y quieren que haga bien los exámenes. Claro, yo también quiero sacar buenas notas.

Second paragraph

The second paragraph introduces another idea – in this example it discusses different ways to combat stress, which allows the discussion to move towards hobbies and interests. This creates an opportunity to add relevant details and expand the idea. Using the correct reflexive pronoun of the reflexive verb *relajarse* shows a good command of reflexive verbs.

Por eso, para relajarme me gusta hacer varias cosas como leer, ver películas o series, escuchar música o hacer deporte. Practico el ciclismo dos o tres veces a la semana y voy en bicicleta sola o con mis amigas. Por supuesto, uso las redes sociales para mantenerme conectada, pero intento usar mi móvil solo dos horas al día.

Third paragraph

The third and final paragraph adds further detail – in the example the speaker moves to discuss healthy eating. Use this paragraph to bring in a change of tense – here the perfect (*hemos aprendido*) is given – and again this will bring impressive variety to your use of verbs.

Desde mi punto de vista, llevar una vida sana es muy importante para los jóvenes ya que ayuda con el equilibrio. Intento comer sano y recientemente mis amigas y yo hemos aprendido a cocinar platos más saludables. Sin embargo, nos gusta comer la comida rápida de vez en cuando – es normal, ¿no?

Pronunciation

When you learn new words in Spanish, it is important that you learn how to say them as well as how to write them. This will mean you speak confidently in your performance.

The conversation

In the conversation section of the exam you will be able to use prepared material and adapt it to respond to the questions from your teacher/lecturer. You will also need to use or adapt vocabulary and phrases you hear in the questions. This is what is known as 'manipulating the language'.

You will need to have the confidence to use and adapt material you have learned and practised during the course. It is essential that you practise both in class and at home.

> ### Hints & tips ⭐
>
> ✓ Check pronunciation with your teacher/lecturer.
> ✓ Use online support for pronunciation.
> ✓ Say the words out loud – you can even record yourself – and then compare yourself to online/teacher/lecturer pronunciation.

Practice

Think of a conversation you have had recently in English.
● How did you respond to questions?
● Did you have thinking time before responding?
● Think of what made the conversation 'natural'.

Reflect on the points above, and try to apply these to your conversation in Spanish.

Hints & tips ⭐

Grammatical accuracy is important to gain higher marks. For example:

✓ *familiarity with verb forms, e.g. the ability to switch from the first person singular (I) to the third person singular (he/she). For example:*
'Tengo una familia grande: dos hermanos y dos hermanas. Mi hermano mayor se llama David y tiene 20 años'.

✓ *accuracy with adjectival agreements. For example:*
'En general, creo que mis amigas son listas e intentan trabajar mucho en el instituto. Del mismo modo, mis hermanos son muy trabajadores a la hora de estudiar'.

Hints & tips ⭐

To help you manage your answers in the conversation, the following suggestions can help you:

✓ *Use introductory words/phrases to give you thinking time to respond to questions — these also make your replies appear more natural. For example, in reply to '¿Adónde fuiste de vacaciones el año pasado?', say:*
'Pues, a ver, el año pasado mi familia y yo visitamos el sur de Inglaterra'.

✓ *Use variation in your responses — as a rule, try not to always talk about yourself! Apart from being a little one dimensional, it also only shows your teacher/lecturer that you can use the first-person singular (the 'I' part) verb. Show that you can use more. For example, by talking about yourself and other people, you can use the first-person plural (the 'we' part) verb: 'mi familia y yo'; 'mis amigos y yo'; 'mi hermano menor y yo'.*

Below is an example of a conversation based on the context of **employability**. In the following grid are example questions and suggested ways of how to develop the answers.

¿Tienes un trabajo a tiempo parcial?	For these types of questions ('Do you have...?', 'Are you...?' etc.), don't just answer *Sí* or *No*! If your answer is *Sí*, expand and give details. Here you could talk about what type of job, your part-time job is, where you work, what days (and times) you work, your opinion of it, what you earn and what you spend it on:
	Sí, trabajo de camarero en un café. Trabajo los sábados de nueve a cinco y me gusta mucho porque es variado. Gano 40 libras y gasto mi dinero en ropa y música.
	If your answer is *No*, you can expand as follows:
	No, no tengo un trabajo a tiempo parcial en este momento porque tengo que estudiar mucho para mis exámenes.

¿Qué haces para ganar dinero?	This is an open type of question, allowing you to put in as much detail as you can. For example, you could talk about what tasks about the house you do to earn money, how often and who pays you etc.
	Remember the previous advice about variation – try to use other parts of the verb or even other tenses:
	Pues, tengo que ayudar en casa, por ejemplo cargo el lavaplatos todas las tardes y paso la aspiradora por mi habitación los fines de semana. No me gusta mucho, pero mi madre me paga 20 libras – ¡qué bien! Sin embargo, mi hermana no hace mucho en casa porque solo tiene nueve años.
En el futuro, ¿qué tipo de trabajo quieres hacer?	This question allows you to use other tenses, namely the present, the future and the conditional tenses, so it introduces some variation in language. Remember to give a reason too as to the type of job you would like to do:
	En el futuro me gustaría ser científico porque se me dan bien las ciencias y creo que sería muy interesante. Iré a la universidad para estudiar química y física.
	Equally, if you are not sure what job you would like to do in the future, you could answer as follows:
	Pues, la verdad es que no sé qué quiero hacer en el futuro. Voy a hacer un sexto curso y luego decidiré.
¿Te gustaría trabajar en el extranjero?	You could mention here the country or countries you would like to visit and work in and discuss why working abroad attracts you (or not).
	Sí, creo que sería una buena idea tener experiencia de vivir y trabajar en otro país. Quizás me gustaría trabajar en los Estados Unidos para aprender más sobre su cultura.
¿Has hecho tus prácticas laborales?	In this answer you can give details about your work experience (where you worked, what it was like, the tasks you had to do, your work colleagues etc.). You could use some of the material you prepare for the bullet point in the writing – question paper around 'related work experience':
	Sí, trabajé en un gabinete de abogados donde tuve que archivar documentos y contestar el teléfono. Fue muy divertido y conocí a mucha gente nueva. Mis compañeros y yo nos llevamos muy bien.

Writing

Throughout the National 5 Spanish course, you will have many opportunities to write about things that interest you or that are relevant to you. These topics should be related to the broad contexts of **society**, **learning**, **employability** and **culture**.

Hints & tips ★

Write about things that are familiar to you or interest you from the SQA list of contexts, topics and suggested development of topics (see page vii). It is easier (and more enjoyable) to write about things you are interested in as you will have more to say and you will be able to give more details.

You will develop the skill of writing through preparing for the talking activities and the writing tasks (both the job e-mail in Question paper 1 and the writing assignment). In addition, learning vocabulary (see Chapter 9) and revising grammar (see Chapter 8) will develop further accuracy in your writing skills.

For the writing tasks, structure your pieces in the same way as you did for the talking presentation and break them down into three paragraphs. This will help with both developing your ideas and remembering the content.

Hints & tips

✓ Try to write about things that are familiar to you or interest you.

✓ Spelling and accuracy are key – learning vocabulary on a regular basis will help with both.

✓ It is a good idea to re-draft work corrected by your teacher/lecturer so you have a corrected copy – this also helps you learn from any changes suggested.

✓ Use a range of sources to help you, but don't copy large chunks if you don't understand them.

✓ Use your dictionary to help with checking of spelling.

✓ As for the preparation for talking, make sure you have variation in your language: verb tenses, parts of verbs, a good range of adjectives and adverbs.

✓ Avoid listing words – this does not show variety. Give two or three examples instead, and expand on some of these.

✓ Use a variety of opinion words and phrases when writing about what you think about something.

✓ Avoid more simple structures – you will get better marks for correct use of more complex structures for National 5 level.

Practice

Writing in Spanish should allow you to show the vocabulary and grammatical structures you know with a very good degree of accuracy.

● How can you expand basic sentences?
● What other details would add interest?
● How many ways can you show your knowledge of Spanish and your ability to use a wide range of grammatical structures?

Remember these points as you prepare your writing in Spanish.

The following are examples of two types of writing you may do for National 5 Spanish: personal writing and discursive writing.

Personal writing: your subjects/studies

The following example could be used for the talking presentation, or it could be expanded on for the writing assignment. The extracts could be adapted to address the bullet point in the job advert stimulus (school/college/education experience until now).

First paragraph

In the first section, introduce the topic and give your opinion of school.

Mis estudios

Desde mi perspectiva, mi instituto es bastante bueno porque tengo muchos amigos allí y en general me gustan las asignaturas que estudio. Tenemos suerte, porque el instituto ofrece una variedad de actividades diferentes, como por ejemplo una variedad de deportes, un club de teatro y viajes extraescolares.

Second paragraph

Introduce a new idea. Go on to write about your subjects. Don't just list what you study; instead, write about what you need to study at school and what subjects you have chosen to do (and why). Add detail to access higher marks. Include opinions and write about which subjects you are good at and which ones you are not so strong at.

Estoy en cuarto, y estudio cinco asignaturas: el inglés y las matemáticas son obligatorias, y he elegido estudiar biología, teatro y español. Me encanta el teatro porque me ayuda a relajarme y en el futuro quizás me gustaría trabajar en algo relacionado con el teatro. Desafortunadamente, no me se dan bien las mates: tengo que hacer muchos deberes en casa pero mi profesor es bueno: explica muy bien y me ayuda si tengo un problema.

Third paragraph

Use the third and final paragraph to write about your plans for studying, for example in high school, at college or at university. This also allows you to use other tenses, such as the conditional (what you would like to do) and the future (what you are going to do/what you will do).

Después del quinto/sexto curso espero ir a la universidad para seguir estudiando teatro. Tendré que sacar buenas notas en mis exámenes. Me gustaría compartir un piso con mis amigos porque quiero independizarme más. En mi opinión, ¡sería fenomenal vivir en el centro de la ciudad! Y después de mis estudios, mis amigos y yo podríamos viajar por el mundo y explorar otros países.

Discursive writing: the use of digital technology

This type of writing will allow you present your opinions and feelings on the subject, as well as compare what others think. You can use a range of opinion phrases here and content from sources you use in class and at home.

Look at the example below and see what relevant material you could use and/or adapt in your writing. You need to also think about how you will structure it: again, it is best to go for three sections.

First paragraph

Introduce the topic and give your opinion of using technology. Include details, such as what you use and when you use it.

La tecnología hoy en día

Creo que la tecnología hoy en día es fundamental. Yo la uso todos los días, como la mayoría de los jóvenes de mi edad. Uso el móvil para conectarme con mis amigos, usando las redes sociales. En general, paso unas tres horas cada día: leo mensajes de mis amigos y miro fotos de la gente famosa (actores y cantantes). También, para hacer mis deberes, uso el portátil en casa. Prefiero hacer mis deberes en línea porque es más fácil cambiar cosas, y puedo investigar temas escolares.

Second paragraph

Write about the advantages and disadvantages of technology and include what other people think of it.

Por supuesto, hay muchas ventajas de usar la tecnología. Tienes mucha información disponible y puedes buscar detalles con rapidez. También, es fácil estar al día de todo lo que pasa en el mundo. Sin embargo, hay peligros importantes y tienes que saber utilizar bien la tecnología. Es importante cambiar con regularidad tus contraseñas y mantener tu perfil privado en las redes sociales para evitar acoso y problemas de seguridad. Mi madre se preocupa mucho de mi seguridad en línea pero siempre uso la tecnología con cuidado.

Third paragraph

In the last section give more detail about your opinions and include some more detailed language and structures. Use another tense (this example uses the preterite).

Ayer, leí en una página web que un 78% de los jóvenes admiten que no podrían vivir sin sus teléfonos móviles. En mi opinión, necesito mi móvil pero también sé que tengo que pasar tiempo sin él. Intento hacer un poco de deporte todos los días y claro, ¡es más interesante hablar con tus amigos cara a cara!

Grammar

In assessing your talking and writing skills, your teacher/lecturer and SQA markers will expect accuracy in your Spanish. In this chapter we have looked at ways to make your talking and writing more varied, using a wider range of structures, verbs and tenses. In addition, there is an expectation that your basic grammar will be accurate so you should make sure you know and use the following points of grammar correctly.

Verbs

- Use the correct forms of the verb. Remember that in Spanish the use of the subject pronouns (*yo, tú, él, ella, nosotros, vosotros, ellos* and *ellas*) is optional or to avoid confusion. Remember to check that you have used the correct verb ending and the correct tense.
- You should ensure that you can use the present, preterite, imperfect, future and conditional tenses.
- Remember that when making a verb negative in Spanish you should put the word *no* before the verb. Remember also that *nunca* (never) can go before the verb or after the verb but with *no* before it. For example, *Nunca como chocolate* or *No como nunca chocolate* (I never eat chocolate).
- Reflexive verbs require the use of a reflexive pronoun. The reflexive pronoun generally goes before the verb, although it can go after the verb in situations such as the future with 'going to' or after a structure such as *tener que*. For example, *Me voy a preparar bien para mis exámenes* or *Voy a prepararme bien para mis exámenes* (I'm going to prepare well for my exams).
- Make sure you know modal verbs such as *poder* (to be able to) and *deber* (to have to).

Nouns

- When you learn vocabulary, make sure you learn the gender of the words: masculine or feminine. You should also ensure you know the correct spelling of plural words.
- Some nouns change meaning depending on the gender: for example, *el capital* (masculine) refers to capital (money) but *la capital* (feminine) refers to the capital city of a country.

Pronouns

- Ensure that you know the correct position of pronouns (object and reflexive) and can use emphatic pronouns. For example, the reflexive pronoun comes before the verb in the present, perfect, preterite, future and conditional tenses.
- When you use 'going to' or a modal verb such as *querer* (to want) or *poder* (to be able) you can place the reflexive pronoun before the main verb or after the infinitive: *Me voy a duchar* or *Voy a ducharme* (I'm going to have a shower); *Me puedo organizar* or *Puedo organizarme* (I can organise myself).

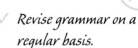

Hints & tips

✓ *Revise grammar on a regular basis.*
✓ *Check you can identify and use correctly a range of tenses.*
✓ *Practice can make perfect – use online as well as textbook grammar support and exercises.*
✓ *Check your written work carefully – look at spelling, verbs and agreements.*

Adjectives

- Most adjectives you will use go after the noun they are describing. Make sure adjectives agree with the noun (masculine/feminine/ singular/plural).
- Watch out for *grande* – it may appear before a noun (meaning 'great') and its spelling changes: for example, *Gran Bretaña* (Great Britain).

For better grades, you will have to do more than this. The language resource column in the table on pages 61–63 and 67 in Chapters 6 and 7 shows what SQA markers are going to be looking for. When you are working through the talking and writing chapters, it will be useful to refer to these pages sometimes so that you can show off your knowledge of Spanish to the SQA marker.

In the exam you will be assessed on your reading skills. This is your ability to understand written information in Spanish and show this understanding by answering questions in English.

There are three texts in the reading question paper: Texts 1, 2 and 3. The text is usually a short article (for example, from a newspaper) on which you will answer a series of questions. The questions for each text are worth 10 marks, so the total for this paper is 30 marks.

Before each text there is a short introduction in English, and a photo/graphic with each text.

The reading texts will be on three of the four contexts. The fourth context will be assessed in the listening paper. For example, if the reading texts are on the contexts on **society**, **culture** and **learning**, then the listening text will be based on the context of **employability**. Of course, this can change each year.

How to read – and answer questions

Following each text there will be a series of questions to test your ability to understand written Spanish. Use the following tips to help you when answering the questions:

1   **Read** the short introduction in English to give you an idea of what the text is about.
2   **Look** over the questions in English that follow the text – these will give you an idea of what information you are being asked to find. It is also useful to circle or underline the questions words (for example, 'what…?' or 'why…?'). You will also have hook words in each question which will relate back to words in the text – these act as 'signposts' to where the answers will be found.
3   **Skim** through the text. This will allow you to start identifying areas where possible answers to the questions may be found. On your question paper you can circle or underline words or sentences that may be useful when answering.
4   Now **answer** the questions – and remember those 'signposts'!

Questions

The questions will be in order of where the information comes in the text. For example, the information required to answer question 2 will appear after the information for question 1, and so on.

There will be different types of question. For example, you might be asked to write out information, fill in the blank(s), say whether a statement is

Hints & tips

In the exam you will be given the reading question paper and the writing question paper at the same time. You have 90 minutes for both question papers. Ideally you should allocate about 1 hour to the reading section so you need to ensure you know how to identify the correct material in a Spanish text, how to answer succinctly and correctly, and take 1 or 2 minutes left to check answers over before going on to the writing section.

Hints & tips

The signposts or 'hook' words are the words in the Spanish text that relate to wording in a question. These then help you to identify where the answer to the question may be found. For example, in the first reading text below you have the following question:

✓ *According to the article, what do almost 80% of Spanish students suffer from during the school year? Give details.*   1

In the Spanish text you find the number ochenta, *so 80% in the question is acting as the hook word.*

true or false, or complete a table. You will find examples of all types of questions in the practice exercises in this chapter.

Timing

You have 1.5 hours to complete the reading and writing paper. It is important to use the time wisely and not spend too long (or too little time) on each of the sections. Aim to allocate about 1 hour to the reading section. It is crucial to practise this timing technique as you get nearer to the final exam by working on past papers.

How to answer

The following is an example reading text to show you how to practise finding answers and how to write your answers. Look at the following example text and questions after it:

You read a report into the health of students in Spain.

Informe sobre la salud entre los estudiantes de 14 a 18 años

Según el Instituto de Salud Pública Español (ISPE), casi el 80 por ciento de los estudiantes españoles sufre de algún dolor o síntomas de malestar durante el año escolar. Por una parte, los dolores de cabeza son muy comunes, a veces provocados por la presión escolar, por pasar mucho tiempo delante del ordenador o porque les gusta hacer deberes por más de dos horas. El dolor de cabeza suele aparecer acompañado de nauseas y dolor de ojos.

La mitad de los estudiantes también tienen problemas físicos como dolor de espalda, hombros, rodillas, pies y piernas. Esto podría ser debido a las tres clases de educación física que los estudiantes tienen durante la semana.

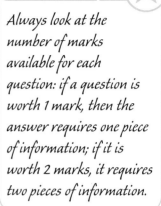

Always look at the number of marks available for each question: if a question is worth 1 mark, then the answer requires one piece of information; if it is worth 2 marks, it requires two pieces of information.

Questions

1   According to the article, what do almost 80% of Spanish students suffer from during the school year? Give details.   **1**

    ....

'Almost 80%' is a translation of *casi el 80 por ciento* so you know you can find the information **after** this phrase.

'During the school year' is *durante el año escolar* so the information you need will come **before** this phrase. The information you are looking for is: *algún dolor o síntomas de malestar*.

Answer: pain or symptoms of feeling unwell (or pain or symptoms of discomfort/unease).

'Give details' in the question means you need to provide all of the above for the 1-mark answer.

Hints & tips

Remember the tips on how to use the dictionary in Chapter 1 (page 2). When you look up malestar there will be at least three translations – use the context (the topic of the article, the information you have in the short introduction in English and in the questions) to arrive at the best translation.

Hints & tips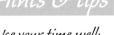

Use your time well:

✓ *Don't re-write the question in your answer.*
✓ *Write the answer directly and clearly.*
✓ *You don't need to write in full sentences.*

Question

2   As well as pressure at school, what other reasons are there for headaches? State **two** reasons.   **2**

    ....

The expression *presión escolar* is 'pressure at school' – the information you need to answer the question will follow this phrase. The phrase *provocados por* is similar to the English 'provoked by' or 'caused by'.

The information you need to translate for your answer is: *por pasar mucho tiempo delante del ordenador* and *porque les gusta hacer deberes por más de dos horas*

Answer: spending too much time on the computer and they like doing homework for more than 2 hours.

Hints & tips

Don't waste time re-writing (or paraphrasing) the question. Use the blanks provided to write the information needed to answer the question – don't repeat the question.

Question

3   The article states that half of Spanish students have physical problems. Complete the sentence.   **2**

    This may be due to the three classes of ....
    which the students have ....

The question tells you that the sentence beginning *La mitad de...* contains the information you need. The phrase *Esto podría ser debido a...* introduces the possible reason. In addition, the question gives you the translation of *tres clases de* so this leads you to where the information is.

Therefore, the information you need therefore for your answer is *ejercicio físico* and *durante la semana*.

Answers: physical exercise / during the week

The article continues:

> En la época de exámenes es muy común tener ansiedad y cansancio porque a los estudiantes les interesa sacar buenas notas. El 10 por ciento de los estudiantes de 15 años dicen tener náuseas por la mañana antes de un examen importante, y la mayoría toman paracetamol o aspirinas en casa. En invierno, los catarros y el virus de la gripe afectan al 82 por ciento de los estudiantes, mientras que el 19 por ciento sufren de fiebre y les duele la garganta.

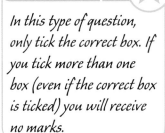
Hints & tips

Watch out for 'ejercicio físico' – this is 'physical exercise' – not 'PE' (which is 'educación física').

Question

4   Why is it common for students to have anxiety and fatigue? Tick (✓) the correct box.   **1**

They want to pass their exams.	
They are interested in getting good results.	
They are interested in writing good notes.	

Hints & tips

In this type of question, only tick the correct box. If you tick more than one box (even if the correct box is ticked) you will receive no marks.

After the phrase *ansiedad y cansancio* the word *porque* will lead you into the answer. *Notas* is the Spanish word for 'results/marks/grades': *les interesa sacar buenas notas*. (The English word 'notes' is translated in Spanish as *apuntes*.)

Answer: second box: they are interested in getting good results.

What you should know

Vocabulary

There are a number of key areas of vocabulary you should aim to familiarise yourself with. Make sure you know these areas before going into the exam as these can arise in reading texts.

You should be familiar with the following:

★ numbers, including prices, dates, times
★ dates, days, seasons, time phrases such as *de vez en cuando, a menudo* etc.
★ common verbs in the present tense such as *ser, estar, decir, ir, tener, hacer*

For useful vocabulary see chapter 9.

Now practise answering questions on each of the four contexts with the following practice texts.

Society

You read an article in a tourist brochure about a town in the north of Spain.

Villaverde de Arriba en festivales

Para muchos turistas extranjeros tanto como españoles, ir de vacaciones significa visitar un lugar de interés y aprender sobre la cultura. Villaverde de Arriba (situado en la provincia de León) puede ofrecer a los turistas una amplia variedad de festivales de todo tipo. De hecho, Villaverde de Arriba cada año alberga una docena de festivales organizados por el Ayuntamiento.

El día 15 de agosto es un día festivo nacional, lo que significa que nadie trabaja y que llegan miles de turistas al pueblo. Este día hay una carrera de tres kilómetros y medio por el Parque Natural de La Fresneda y después de la carrera más de 500 personas comen una paella gigante en la plaza mayor. Además, hay un festival de música alternativa que atrae a personas de todo el mundo. De hecho, el año pasado batió su record de asistencia con más de mil personas.

Natalia Méndez es portavoz del Ayuntamiento y asegura que este año le gustaría aumentar la asistencia a los festivales. "Aunque nuestro pueblo es pequeño, tenemos campings, hoteles y muy buenos restaurantes para los visitantes. Lo que nos hace únicos en Villaverde de Arriba es que damos la bienvenida a todos y tenemos un gran entusiasmo por el turismo".

Questions ?

1 According to the article, what does going on holiday mean for many foreign and Spanish tourists? State any **one** thing.   **1**

....

2 What is Villaverde home to each year?   **1**

....

3 a 15 August is a national festival. According to the article, what does this mean? State **two** things.   **2**

....

....

  b What happens after the race? Complete the sentence.   **2**
    More than .... eat a large paella ....

4 Who does the music festival attract?   **1**

....

5 a What does Natalia Méndez want to do this year?   **1**

....

  b According to Natalia, what makes the inhabitants of Villaverde de Arriba unique? State **two** things.   **2**

....

....

Learning

You read an article about leaving school.

¿Estás en un mar de dudas?

Terminar el curso escolar y empezar una nueva etapa de la vida – esto sí que es emocionante para los jóvenes pero al mismo tiempo puede causarles noches en blanco y problemas de ansiedad. Las opciones son muchas: seguir estudiando, buscar trabajo, tomarse un año sabático o bien hacer un voluntariado.

Por estas razones, y también por haberlo pasado solo hace un par de años, un grupo de jóvenes de Madrid decidió crear una plataforma digital en la cual se puede encontrar toda la información necesaria sobre qué hacer después del instituto. A los estudiantes escolares de toda España les tiende una mano con un sitio web diseñado por jóvenes de su edad para ayudarles a orientar su futuro.

David Bacardit, estudiante de segundo de ingeniería y uno de los creadores de la plataforma, explica que además de dar consejos sobre las opciones que existen, la plataforma también ofrece a los que terminan el instituto ayuda con la parte emocional.

"Al dejar el instituto, yo quería ser más independiente, tenía ganas de vivir en otra ciudad y claro, quería ganarme algo de dinero" dice David. "El problema era que no sabía dónde buscar información". David explica que fue esta la razón por la que decidió ayudar a otros en la misma situación.

Questions ?

1 The article talks about leaving school and starting a new phase in life.
  a What can this cause in young people? State **two** things.   **2**

  ....

  ....

  b What options do young people have? State any **two** options.   **2**

  ....

  ....

2 What did a group of young people in Madrid decide to create?
  a Complete the sentence.   **2**
    They decided to create .... in which you can find
    all the necessary information about ....
  b As well as giving advice, what else does it offer young people who leave school?   **1**

  ....

3 a What did David Bacardit want to do when he left school? State any **two** things.   **2**

  ....

  ....

  b What problem did he have?   **1**

  ....

Employability

You read an article about the young people and jobs.

El trabajo en este mundo en cambio constante

Prepararse para el mundo laboral siempre ha requerido que la gente se formalice, o bien que se prepare a un nivel adecuado para una profesión o un puesto. Sin embargo, hoy en día se hace cada vez más importante que los jóvenes sean flexibles, adaptables y que tengan una variedad de destrezas. Estamos en un mundo laboral de contratos no fijos, contratos de cero horas. De la misma manera, los jóvenes están dispuestos a trabajar en puestos diferentes. El dicho de que un trabajo es de por vida ahora no tiene sentido.

Jaime Muñoz, de 19 años y estudiante de idiomas, es un típico joven español que como muchos otros piensa en su futuro, y cómo le gustaría trabajar al terminar sus estudios. "Por supuesto, trabajar para ganar dinero siempre tendrá importancia", explica Jaime. "Sin embargo, mis amigos y yo también queremos vivir en otros sitios y tener experiencia de otras culturas. No buscamos el trabajo de siempre o tradicional; de hecho, lo importante para mí en mis trabajos del futuro es que pueda viajar y conocer gente nueva".

Es evidente que los jóvenes de hoy no tienen miedo a los contratos temporales porque esta forma de trabajar les resulta ideal para una época de sus vidas en la cual no tienen tantas responsabilidades. Los jóvenes de hoy tienen otras formas de trabajar gracias a la popularidad creciente de trabajar remotamente. La rutina del viaje al trabajo quizás no existirá por mucho tiempo.

Questions ?

1 The article talks about young people and work.
   a According to the article, what is it important for young people to be nowadays? State **three** things. **3**

   ....

   ....

   ....

   b What are young people ready to do? **1**

   ....

2 Jaime Muñoz talks about what he and his friends want.
   a What does he say? Complete the sentence. **2**
      His friends and he want to .... and .... other cultures.
   b According to Jaime, what is important for him in future jobs? State **two** things. **2**

   ....

   ....

3 Why are young people not afraid of fixed-term contracts? Tick (✓) the correct box. **1**

They don't have as many responsibilities at this stage in their lives.	
They can be flexible.	
Not being responsible is ideal.	

4 What may not exist for much longer? **1**

   ....

Culture

You read an article about tourism in Uruguay.

El turismo uruguayo

Un informe publicado ayer destaca que Uruguay recibió casi 4 millones de turistas el año pasado, lo cual representa el 98 por ciento de su población. No hay duda de que esta cifra demuestra claramente la importancia del sector turístico en la economía uruguaya. Aparte del turismo, otras fuentes importantes de exportación son el ganado y los recursos minerales.

La gran mayoría de los turistas vienen de Argentina y Brasil (los dos países vecinos de Uruguay) y recientemente el gobierno ha empezado una campaña publicitaria para atraer a más turistas de Europa. Para conseguir esto, el gobierno ha invertido mucho dinero en el sector turístico y también ha permitido la construcción de nuevos hoteles.

Isabel Andrés, ministra del Departamento de Turismo y directora de la nueva campaña, asegura que en Uruguay han desarrollado la infraestructura hotelera y cuentan con servicios turísticos de calidad. "Las principales atracciones son el variado paisaje natural junto al aspecto cultural" explica Isabel. "De cultura, tenemos El Carnaval de Montevideo que es uno de los más largos del mundo: se extiende durante todo el mes de febrero y la primera mitad de marzo". Isabel describe que durante los días del Carnaval, las calles se llenan de desfiles y de gente alegre. También, además de bailes tradicionales, durante los últimos días del Carnaval el Ayuntamiento de Montevideo organiza concursos de disfraces.

Questions ?

1 a Nearly 4 million tourists visited Uruguay last year. What does this figure represent? Give details.   **1**

   ....

   b There are two other important exports for Uruguay. State any **one** of them.   **1**

   ....

2 a What has the government done recently? Complete the sentence.   **2**
      It has started a .... to attract ....
   b What has the government done to achieve this? State any **one** thing.   **1**

   ....

3 a What does Isabel Andrés say are important attractions? State **two** things.   **2**

   ....

   ....

   b When does the Carnival take place? State **two** details.   **2**

   ....

   ....

   c As well as traditional dances, what else does the Town Hall organise?   **1**

   ....

Chapter 3 Answers for reading tasks

Society

1 visiting a place of interest; learning about culture (any one)
2 a dozen festivals
3 a nobody works; thousands of tourists arrive
   b 500 people/in the main square)
4 people from all over the world
5 a Increase attendance at all the festivals
   b welcome everyone; have great enthusiasm for tourism

Learning

1 a sleepless nights; problems with anxiety
   b continue/keep studying; look for work/a job; have a gap year; do volunteer work (any two)
2 a a digital platform; what to do after (leaving) school
   b help with the emotional side
3 a be more independent; live in another city; earn some money (any two)
   b he didn't know where to look for information

Employability

1 a flexible; adaptable, have a range of skills
   b work in different jobs
2 a live in different places; experience
   b travel; meet new people
3 First box. They don't have as many responsibilities at this stage in their lives.
4 the routine of travelling to work

Culture

1 a 98% of the population
   b livestock; minerals (any one)
2 a publicity campaign; more tourists from Europe
   b invested lots of money in the tourist sector; allowed building of new hotels (any one)
3 a varied natural scenery/landscapes; cultural side
   b all of February; first half of March
   c fancy dress competitions

Listening

In the exam you will be assessed on your listening skills. This is **listening for information** – assessing your familiarity with the vocabulary associated with the four contexts. The listening paper has a total mark allocation of 20 marks, which is 25% of the final mark.

The context for the listening paper will be the one that is **not** in the reading question paper. For example, if the reading paper covers the contexts of **society**, **culture** and **learning**, then the listening Items will be based on the context of **employability**. Of course, this can change each year.

There are **two** parts to the listening paper: a monologue and a conversation.
- **Monologue**: one speaker talks in Spanish for approximately 1 minute. You will hear this three times, with an interval of 1 minute each time and then you have to answer questions about what has been said. There are 8 marks available for this part of the listening exam.
- **Conversation:** this is a short conversation in Spanish between two speakers that lasts for approximately 2 minutes. You will also hear this three times, with an interval of 1 minute each time. There are 12 marks available for this part of the listening exam.

Between the monologue and the conversation there is a pause of 2 minutes for you to look over your answers. At the end of the conversation you will have 5 minutes to look over all your answers for both the monologue and the conversation.

Before each, you are given 1 minute to read the questions. This will give you an idea of the context and the topic covered before you start to listen.

You will hear vocabulary that won't be needed to answer the questions, so it is important to read the questions carefully before you listen for the first time, as it can be tempting to write everything down.

> ### Hints & tips
>
> *You have 1 minute to read the questions before you listen to each section. Use this time to read the questions carefully and think about the possible vocabulary that you may hear.*

Hints & tips

Always look at the number of marks for each question: if a question is worth 1 mark, then the answer will require one piece of information; if it is worth 2 marks, it will require two pieces of information.

Practice

When watching a Spanish film/TV programme or listening to a Spanish podcast or the radio, or even when doing a listening activity in your class, try to note:
- what the topic is
- 2 or 3 key points you understand
- 1 or 2 opinions (if any) of the people speaking

This will help you develop the skill of listening for information.

Look at the following example question:

Question

What does Elena think about technology? State any **one** thing.　　　1

....

This question implies that Elena is talking about her opinion of technology, and because the question says 'state any **one** thing' you know she will say at least two opinions. Elena actually said:

Creo que la tecnología es muy importante para los jóvenes, y ayuda con la comunicación.

So, the answer to the question for 1 mark would be either 'It is important for young people.' or 'It helps with communication.'

Hints & tips

Familiarise yourself with the types of question that might come up. You may be asked to fill in the blank, decide whether a statement is true or false, or complete a table.

How to listen – and write your answers

Once you have read the questions carefully, and you have thought about possible vocabulary you may hear, you will then hear the recording three times. The exam requires you to read the questions, listen to the monologue/dialogue and write your answers, so there is a lot for you to do.

When you listen for the first time, write your answers as short notes at the left side of the question. Then, when you listen the second and third times, you can check whether your first answer is correct, and if you are happy that it is, cross out your note and write your answer clearly in the space provided in the question paper.

What you should know

Vocabulary

Across each of the four contexts you will need to learn and revise the vocabulary you learn in class that is specific to each context and topics (see Chapter 9). In addition, you will need to revise regularly the following as they often appear in Listening transcripts:

★ numbers, including prices, dates, times
★ days of the week, months and seasons of the year
★ members of the family
★ prepositions (e.g. in front of, next to, near etc.)
★ opinion phrases (*me gusta, me encanta, prefiero*)

Hints & tips

Look out for 'hook words' in the question. These help you identify when the information you need for an answer is coming up. In the example above, 'What does Elena think about technology? State any one thing', the hook word is 'think' – you need to listen out for her opinion and what that is. The opinion phrase creo que ('I think that…') leads you into the information required for the answer.

Hints & tips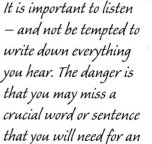

It is important to listen – and not be tempted to write down everything you hear. The danger is that you may miss a crucial word or sentence that you will need for an answer.

Practice monologues

In the monologue, one speaker talks in Spanish about a topic based on a context. There are 8 marks available for this section.

There will be a variety of question types, requiring you to give an answer, complete a sentence (fill in the blank) or complete a table.

WWW

Audio files for the listening tasks are available to download here:

www.hoddergibson.co.uk/audio-how-to-pass-spanish.

Practice 1: Society

🔊 *Elena talks about technology. Listen to what she says and then answer the questions.*

Questions ❓

1 Elena says that, like many young people of her age, she uses technology. What does she use her mobile for? State any **two** things.   **2**

....

....

2 She says she tries to have a balance in her life. Complete the sentence.

I don't use my mobile phone after .... so I can .... better.   **2**

3 What does she do during the week? State any **one** thing.   **1**

....

4 Elena says her mother works from home sometimes.
   a How often does her mother work from home?   **1**

....

   b Why does her mother prefer to shop online than go to the supermarket? State any **one** reason.   **1**

....

5 What can she do if she finds a problem? State **one** thing.   **1**

....

Practice 2: Learning

🔊 *Natalia talks about her school. Listen to what she says and then answer the questions.*

Questions ❓

1 How far is Natalia's school from her house?   **1**

....

2 As well as normal classes, there are many things to do at her school. Complete the sentence.   **2**

You can learn .... and there is an art club at ....   ➡

3 Natalia talks about learning online.
  a Why does she think this is a good thing? State any **two** reasons.   **2**

    ....

    ....

  b Where can pupils rent tablets from?   **1**

    ....

4 Natalia talks about studying history and geography. What does she say? Tick (✓) the correct statement.   **1**

They have always interested her, and they are practical.	
She thinks they are interesting and useful.	
They have always interested her, and they are informative.	

5 She talks about the future. What area would she like to work in?   **1**

    ....

Practice 3: Employability

🔊 *Javier talks about his part-time job. Listen to what he says and then answer the questions.*

Questions ❓

1 What does Javier study at university?   **1**

    ....

2 When does he prefer to take the bus to university? State any **one** thing.   **1**

    ....

3 Javier has a part-time job on a Saturday.
  a Where does he work?   **1**

    ....

  b Where exactly is it situated? State **two** things.   **2**

    ....

    ....

4 He talks about the tasks he does in his job. What does he say is the best thing about them?
State any **one** thing.   **1**

    ....

5 According to Javier, what is it important to do? Complete the sentence.   **2**

    It is important to .... and plan ....

Practice 4: Culture

🔊 *Tomás talks about watching films. Listen to what he says and then answer the questions.*

Questions ?

1 Tomás talks about how he normally watches films. Complete the sentence.　　**1**

He prefers to watch films and series on his tablet because he can decide ....
he watches them.

2 **a** What type of film does he like to watch? State any **one** type.　　**1**

....

b Why is this? State any **one** reason.　　**1**

....

3 Tomás talks about his nearest cinema. How does he describe it? State any **two** things.　　**2**

....

....

4 He went to the cinema with his friend last Saturday. What did they do before the film? State **two** things.　　**2**

....

....

5 What opportunity does Tomás believe the cinema provides?　　**1**

....

Practice conversations

In the conversation, one speaker asks the other speaker questions in Spanish about a topic based on a context (the same context as the monologue). There are 12 marks available for this section.

There may be a variety of question types: ones that require an answer, those asking you to complete a sentence (fill in the blank) or those asking you to complete a table.

Practice 1: Society

🔊 *Sara talks to José about keeping fit and healthy. Listen to what they say and then answer the questions.*

Questions ?

1 Sara talks about what she does at the sports centre. Tick (✓) the **two** correct statements.　　**2**

She does half an hour of exercise.	
She likes a variety of activities.	
She goes swimming three times per week.	
She goes to the sports centre three times a week.	

➜

2 Sara thinks she leads a healthy life. What does she say? Complete the sentence. **2**

Leading a healthy life makes you .... and it helps with

....

3 She then talks about what she does to lead a healthy life.
   a What exactly does she do? **1**

   ....

   b How often does she do this? **1**

   ....

   c What does she say about her eating habits? State any **two** things. **2**

   ....

   ....

4 Sara speaks about her family.
   a What is her sister's opinion of fast food? **1**

   ....

   b What does Sara say about her brother's eating habits? **1**

   ....

5 In what ways does Sara say that school helps her lead a healthy lifestyle? State **two** things. **2**

   ....

   ....

Practice 2: Learning

Almudena talks to Ignacio about a recent school trip to Scotland.
Listen to what they say and then answer the questions.

Questions ?

1 Almudena returned last night from a school trip to Edinburgh. Why is she tired today? **1**

   ....

2 She speaks about the accommodation. Where did Almudena and the other pupils and teachers stay?
State **two** things. **2**

   ....

   ....

3 She talks about their first day in the school.
   a What did they do in the morning? **1**

   ....

   b What did they do in the afternoon? State any **one** thing. **1**

   ....

4 What does she say about the Scottish teachers? State any **two** things. **2**

   ....

   ....

5 Almudena talks about the differences between Spanish and Scottish schools. What does she say is the biggest difference for her? **1**

....

6 Almudena says they visited many places during the trip to Scotland.
  a What did they do on the last day? State **two** things. **2**

....

....

  b What was her favourite experience? **1**

....

7 What is going to happen next year? **1**

....

Practice 3: Employability

🔊 *Esteban talks to Cristina about his new part-time job in a supermarket. Listen to what they say and then answer the questions.*

Questions ❓

1 What does Esteban say about his new job? State any **one** thing. **1**

....

2 Esteban describes how he found his job in the supermarket. Complete the sentence below. **2**

He spent a lot of time online .... and he joined a ....

3 He talks about his job interview. What did he say about his personal qualities? State any **two** things. **2**

....

....

4 Esteban describes his work hours.
  a What time does he start? **1**

....

  b How long does he have for lunch? **1**

....

  c What does he think of the cafeteria food? State any **one** thing. **1**

....

5 Esteban fills the supermarket shelves.
  a What does he say about this? State any **one** thing. **1**

....

  b When does he help the customers? State any **one** thing. **1**

....

6 What has Esteban learned from working at the supermarket? State any **two** things. **2**

....

....

Practice 4: Culture

🔊 *María talks to Javier about a recent holiday with her family. Listen to what they say and then answer the questions.*

Questions ?

1 Where exactly did María go on holiday?　　　　　　　　　　　　　　　　　**1**

....

2 María stayed in a four-star hotel with her family. Where was it situated? Complete the sentence.　**2**

The hotel was situated in ...., only .... from the beach.

3 María describes what they could do in the hotel.

    a What could they do during the day? State any **two** things.　　　　　　**2**

....

....

    b What does María say about the hotel staff? State any **one** thing.　　　　**1**

....

4 **a** What did they normally do after breakfast?　　　　　　　　　　　　**1**

....

    b Why does María think it is better to visit the tourist sites in the morning?　**1**

....

5 **a** In general, how did María get on with her family during the holiday?　　**1**

....

    b She says they sometimes argued. What does she say about this? State any **one** thing.　**1**

....

6 María says she will study in Ireland during next year's holiday. What does she say she will do there? State **two** things.　　　　　　　　　　　　　　　　**2**

....

....

Transcripts and answers for listening tasks

Practice monologues

Practice 1: Society

Elena talks about technology.

Tengo que decir que la tecnología es muy importante para los jóvenes. Como muchas personas de mi edad, uso mi móvil para charlar con mis amigos, para ver series y también para leer en las redes sociales. La verdad es que no veo mucho la televisión; prefiero ver programas o películas en mi tablet porque es más práctico. Creo que tienes más control con la tablet que con la televisión. Sin embargo, intento tener un equilibrio en mi vida y no uso el móvil después de las diez de la noche para poder dormir bien. Durante la semana, practico deporte tres veces a la semana y salgo a menudo con mis amigos para hablar cara a cara.

Hoy en día casi todo el mundo usa la tecnología de una forma u otra. Por ejemplo, mi madre trabaja en una empresa y pasa tres días a la semana teletrabajando, o sea, trabajando desde casa. También, mi madre prefiere hacer la compra en línea que ir al supermercado porque dice que es más fácil y más rápido.

Claro que hay desventajas y es importante tener cuidado. Si encuentro algún problema, puedo hablar con mi madre porque tenemos una buena relación y confía en mí. Afortunadamente, pienso que, en general, estamos aprendiendo a usar la tecnología de forma más segura.

Answers

1 chat to friends; watch series; read social media (any two)
2 10 o'clock/sleep
3 plays sport; goes out with friends (any one)
4 a 3 days per week
  b easier; quicker (any one)
5 speak to her mum

Practice 2: Learning

Natalia talks about her school.

Tengo que decir que voy a un instituto muy bueno. Es un instituto de unos mil alumnos y está a diez minutos andando de mi casa. Como a mí me encanta el deporte, lo bueno de mi instituto es que tienes muchas instalaciones deportivas: hay una pista de tenis, un campo de fútbol y una piscina. Aparte de las clases normales, siempre hay algo que hacer: por ejemplo, se puede aprender bailes tradicionales y hay un club de dibujo a la hora de comer. Antes de empezar mis clases por la mañana, nado con el equipo de natación del instituto. Empezamos a las seis y media y entrenamos una hora. Ahora estoy acostumbrada a levantarme temprano pero siempre es más difícil en invierno.

Aparte del trabajo que hacemos en clase, tenemos que trabajar en línea haciendo tareas o proyectos. Aprender en línea me parece bueno porque puedes colaborar digitalmente y compartir ideas más fácilmente. Los profesores corrigen el trabajo y te dejan mensajes sobre lo que tienes que hacer para mejorar. No hay ningún problema si no tienes ordenador en casa porque los alumnos pueden alquilar una tablet de la biblioteca del instituto.

Este año he decidido estudiar ocho asignaturas, incluyendo historia y geografía porque siempre me han interesado, y en mi opinión son informativas. Quizás iré a la universidad a estudiar algo relacionado con la geografía. Creo que necesitamos hacer más para proteger el planeta así que, en el futuro, me gustaría trabajar en algo relacionado con la conservación de los animales.

Answers

1 10 minutes walking/on foot
2 traditional dances; lunchtime
3 a you can collaborate digitally; you can share ideas more easily
   b library
4 Third box. They have always interested her, and they are informative.
5 animal conservation

Practice 3: Employability

Javier talks about his part-time job.

Estoy en mi segundo curso de la universidad donde estudio medicina. La universidad está en las afueras de la ciudad y normalmente voy en bicicleta para hacer un poco de ejercicio. Sin embargo, prefiero coger el autobús a la universidad cuando hace mal tiempo o si llueve, así que tengo que pagar el transporte.

Como muchas personas de mi edad, también tengo un trabajo a tiempo parcial. Es necesario poder pagar mis libros y otras cosas que necesito para mis clases.

Para ganar dinero, trabajo en una tienda de deportes todos los sábados desde las ocho hasta las seis de la tarde. La tienda es bastante grande y está situada en la primera planta de un centro comercial. En un día normal tengo que trabajar en la caja, ayudar a los clientes y limpiar. Lo mejor de hacer estas tareas es que es muy variado y nunca me aburro.

Ahora he empezado a salir con mis compañeros del trabajo los fines de semana. Desde mi punto de vista, es importante organizarse bien y planear el tiempo para estudiar.

Answers

1 medicine
2 bad weather; raining (any one)
3 a in a sports shop
  b first floor; in a shopping centre
4 varied; never gets bored (any one)
5 organise yourself well/be organised; time to study

Practice 4: Culture

Tomás talks about watching films.

Normalmente, prefiero ver las películas y las series en mi tablet porque puedo decidir cuándo las veo.

En general, veo las películas más recientes los viernes o los sábados después de hacer mis tareas de la casa y los deberes. Suelo ver películas románticas o películas de terror porque me interesan y me parecen entretenidas. Sin embargo, mis amigos y yo también vamos al cine una vez al mes. El cine más cercano está a unos veinticinco minutos de nuestro pueblo así que cogemos el tren. Es un cine bastante nuevo con sillas reclinables y una terraza grande.

El sábado pasado fue el cumpleaños de mi mejor amigo así que decidimos celebrarlo yendo al cine. Antes de ver la película, tomamos un refresco en una cafetería y pasamos una hora charlando. Vimos una película de acción recién estrenada y la verdad es que a mí no me pareció muy buena porque era un poco aburrida. No obstante, a mi amigo le encantó.

A pesar de que es muy fácil y muchas veces más cómodo ver películas y programas en la tablet o el móvil, en mi opinión ir al cine también ofrece la oportunidad de disfrutar de una película con otras personas.

Answers

1 when
2 a romantic/love films; horror/scary films
  b they interest him/they are interesting; they are entertaining
3 25 minutes from his town; quite new; has reclining seats; has a large terrace (any two)
4 had a drink (in a café); chatted for an hour
5 enjoy a film with other people

Practice conversations

Practice 1: Society

Sara talks to José about keeping fit and healthy.

José: Hola, Sara. Oye, ¿qué tal?

Sara: Hola José. Muy bien, gracias. Vuelvo del polideportivo y me siento fenomenal.

José: ¿Ah sí? ¿Y qué haces allí?

Sara: Pues, normalmente hago una hora de ejercicio y también paso media hora en la piscina. Me gusta hacer una variedad de actividades. La verdad es que intento ir al polideportivo por lo menos tres veces a la semana.

José: Me parece bien. ¿Crees que llevas una vida sana?

Sara: Bueno, me gusta pensar que sí. Desde mi punto de vista llevar una vida sana te hace feliz y te ayuda con el estrés. Yo intento hacer muchas cosas para llevar una vida sana.

José: Entonces, ¿qué haces exactamente?

Sara: Pues, he empezado a practicar yoga. Lo practico dos veces a la semana. Es normal tener algo de estrés en la vida, pero es importante saber cómo manejarlo. Dado que soy deportista, necesito comer regularmente y comer alimentos que me dan energía y vitaminas. Además, recientemente he aprendido a cocinar platos sanos.

José: ¿Y tu familia también come de manera sana?

Sara: Pues en general, sí. Sin embargo, a mi hermana menor le gusta la comida rápida, pero ella cree que un poco en moderación no está mal. Mi hermano mayor vive en otra ciudad y le gusta cenar en restaurantes diferentes.

José: ¿Qué aprendes en el instituto sobre llevar una vida sana?

Sara: En mi opinión el instituto nos ayuda mucho: puedo hablar con los profesores si tengo problemas de estrés y es obligatorio hacer dos horas por semana de educación física. De hecho, el curso que viene el instituto ofrecerá clases en línea para enseñarnos a cocinar recetas sanas.

José: Me parece estupendo.

Answers

1 Second box. She likes a variety of activities; Fourth box. She goes to the sports centre three times a week.
2 happy; stress
3 a yoga
  b twice a week
  c she eats regularly; she eats things that give her energy and vitamins; she has learned to cook healthy dishes/food (any two)
4 a a little in moderation isn't bad
  b He likes to eat/have dinner in restaurants.
5 she can speak to her teachers (if she is stressed); 2 hours of PE a week; online classes on how to cook healthy recipes (any two)

Practice 2: Learning

Almudena talks to Ignacio about a recent school trip to Scotland.

Ignacio: Hola, Almudena. Oye, acabas de volver de una visita a un instituto en Edimburgo en Escocia con tus compañeros de clase, ¿verdad?

Almudena: Sí, volvimos anoche. La verdad es que hoy estoy cansada porque llegamos a casa a medianoche.

Ignacio: Pues, háblame del viaje. ¿Cómo fue?

Almudena: Bueno, ¡fue una experiencia fenomenal! Viajamos a Edimburgo en avión y los otros alumnos, profesores y yo nos quedamos en un hotel pequeño en las afueras de la ciudad. En total éramos cincuenta y dos alumnos y cuatro profesores en el viaje.

Ignacio: ¡Qué bien! Y, ¿qué hicisteis durante la visita?

Almudena: Pues, la verdad es que fue una visita muy variada. El primer día fuimos al instituto escocés y por la mañana conocimos a los alumnos escoceses. El instituto había organizado un programa muy entretenido para nosotros. Por ejemplo, por la tarde participamos en una clase de educación física y también hicimos una clase de cocina.

Ignacio: ¿Cómo era la gente que conociste?

Almudena: Tengo que decir que todos eran muy simpáticos y nos llevábamos fenomenal. Los profesores escoceses eran muy amables: nos ayudaban mucho y explicaban las cosas muy bien.

Ignacio: Y, ¿crees que hay mucha diferencia entre los institutos españoles y los institutos escoceses?

Almudena: Hombre, ¡claro! Los alumnos en Escocia llevan uniforme y nosotros no. Pero para mí, la diferencia más grande era que en Escocia hay más variedad con las asignaturas y eso me gusta mucho.

Ignacio: ¿Tuvisteis oportunidades de hacer turismo?

Almudena: Sí, visitamos muchos sitios. Por ejemplo, el último día salimos al cine con los alumnos escoceses y después fuimos de compras en el centro de la ciudad. Me hizo mucha ilusión pasar tiempo con los alumnos porque podía practicar el inglés. Tengo que decir que mi experiencia favorita fue aprender los bailes tradicionales – fue muy divertido!

Ignacio: Y ¿crees que vais a mantener el contacto con este instituto escocés?

Almudena: ¡Por supuesto que sí! De hecho, el año que viene los alumnos escoceses vendrán aquí, a España. Ya hemos empezado a pensar en el programa – y me hace mucha ilusión.

Answers

1 She got home at midnight.
2 a small hotel; in the outskirts
3 a met the Scottish pupils
  b took part in a PE class; did a cookery (home economics) class (any one)
4 they were kind; they helped a lot/were very helpful; they explained things well (any two)
5 more variety with subjects
6 a they went to the cinema; went shopping (in city centre)
  b learning traditional dances
7 The Scottish pupils will come to Spain.

Practice 3: Employability

Esteban talks to Cristina about his new part-time job in a supermarket.

Cristina: Hola, Esteban. ¿Qué tal tu nuevo trabajo?

Esteban: Hola, Cristina. Pues la verdad es que me gusta y estoy aprendiendo mucho.

Cristina: Dime, ¿cómo encontraste el puesto?

Esteban: Bueno, pasé mucho tiempo en línea leyendo las ofertas de trabajo y también me apunté a una agencia laboral. Después de tres meses conseguí una entrevista.

Cristina: ¿Y cómo fue la entrevista?

Esteban: En general no estuvo mal. Tuve que contestar una serie de preguntas y hablar con ellos sobre mis cualidades.

Cristina: ¿Ah sí? ¿Y qué dijiste sobre tus cualidades personales?

Esteban: Pues, dije que soy sincero y fiable, y que tengo capacidad de aprender cosas nuevas.

Cristina: ¡Me parece bien! Háblame del trabajo – ¿cómo es tu horario?

Esteban: Bueno, trabajo tres días a la semana – los martes, los jueves y los sábados. Empiezo a las ocho y media y termino a las seis. Normalmente tengo media hora para comer. Suelo comer en la cafetería donde hay un poco de todo: hamburguesas, pastas, ensaladas y bocadillos. En general me encanta porque las raciones son muy grandes.

Cristina: Y ¿qué haces exactamente?

Esteban: Yo trabajo por todo el supermercado rellenando los estantes y esto me mantiene sano y es variado. Por supuesto también ayudo a los clientes si no encuentran lo que buscan, o si tienen una pregunta sobre un producto.

Cristina: ¿Cómo son tus compañeros de trabajo?

Esteban: La verdad es que tengo suerte porque mis dos mejores amigos también trabajan en el supermercado. Los otros compañeros son simpáticos y me ayudan si lo necesito.

Cristina: Y ¿qué has aprendido de trabajar en el supermercado?

Esteban: Pues ahora sé que puedo aprender rápidamente, y que me relaciono bien con los clientes. También me he dado cuenta de que soy trabajador y que me gustan las experiencias nuevas.

Answers

1 he likes it; he's learning a lot (any one)
2 reading job offers/adverts; job agency
3 he's sincere; trustworthy; has capacity to learn new things (any two)
4 a at 8.30
   b half an hour
   c he loves it; the dishes are very big (any one)
5 a it keeps him healthy; it's varied (any one)
   b when they can't find what they're looking for; when they have a question (about a product) (any one)
6 he can learn quickly; he gets on well with the customers; he's hardworking; he likes new experiences (any two)

Practice 4: Culture

María talks to Javier about a recent holiday with her family.

Javier: Hola, María. Dime, ¿qué tal las vacaciones con tu familia?

María: Pues, la verdad es que fenomenal. Acabo de pasar una semana en el sur de Italia con mis padres y mi hermano menor haciendo un montón de actividades.

Javier: ¿Ah sí? ¿Y dónde os alojasteis?

María: Bueno, nos alojamos en un hotel de cuatro estrellas que estaba situado en el centro de la ciudad, a solo quince minutos de la playa.

Javier: ¡Qué bien! Y ¿había mucho que hacer en el hotel?

María: Pues sí. Durante el día podíamos quedarnos en el hotel a jugar al minigolf, tomar clases de cocina o a nadar en la piscina. Y por la noche, después de cenar, mi familia y yo participábamos en concursos organizados por el personal del hotel. El personal era muy amable, nos recibieron muy bien. La verdad es que el hotel tenía de todo.

Javier: ¿Visitaste mucho en la ciudad?

María: La verdad es que todos los días pasábamos dos horas visitando los monumentos de la ciudad. Normalmente, después de desayunar, salíamos del hotel para visitar algún museo. Tengo que admitir que en mi opinión es mejor visitar los sitios turísticos por la mañana porque no hace tanto calor.

Javier: Eso lo entiendo perfectamente. Y tengo que preguntarte – ¿qué tal te llevaste con tu familia?

María: En general, mi familia y yo nos llevamos muy bien durante las vacaciones. Claro, a veces discutíamos pero es normal, ¿no? En mi familia todos somos muy diferentes y tenemos nuestros propios gustos.

Javier: ¿Y ya tienes planes para el año que viene?

María: Pues sí, sé lo que voy a hacer. Pasaré dos semanas estudiando en Irlanda para mejorar mi nivel de inglés y conocer la cultura. ¡Tengo muchas ganas!

Answers

1 south of Italy
2 the city centre; 15 minutes
3 a play mini-golf; take cookery lessons; swim (in the swimming pool) (any two)
   b kind; welcoming (any one)
4 a visit a museum
   b it's not as hot
5 a very well
   b it's normal; they are all different in her family; they all have their own tastes (any one)
6 improve her English; get to know about the culture

Chapter 5

Talking: preparation for the assessment

As you develop your talking skills throughout the National 5 Spanish course, you will prepare in class and at home for the performance–talking part of the exam.

The performance–talking assessment is worth a total of 30 marks. There are two sections: a **presentation** (10 marks) on a topic associated with one of the four contexts, and a **conversation** (20 marks) with your teacher/lecturer. Your teacher/lecturer will first ask you questions based on the context of your presentation and will then ask you questions on one of the other contexts.

For example, if your presentation is the about the context of **learning**, you will be asked some follow-up questions on this context, and then your teacher/lecturer will ask you questions from one of the other three contexts (**society**, **employability** or **culture**).

The presentation section should last approximately 1–2 minutes, and the **conversation** should last 5–6 minutes.

It is important to develop your confidence in talking in Spanish throughout your course as this will help you in the performance–talking. For example, you can develop your confidence in spoken Spanish in class by practising with other learners or by responding to questions in Spanish asked by your teacher/lecturer. At home it is a good idea to practise reading out your Spanish vocabulary aloud. You could record yourself answering questions on your mobile phone.

As you prepare and practise for the performance–talking in class as well as at home, your teacher/lecturer will help you with the two contexts upon which your performance–talking will be based. For example, if your presentation is on your hobbies (from the context of **society**), your follow-up conversation will be on the context of **society** (for example, talking about your hobbies may allow your teacher/lecturer to ask you questions about who you do these with, what you do with your family, how you get on with your family etc.).

Your teacher/lecturer will then ask you some questions from one other context: you and your teacher/lecturer will be able to decide which one would follow on best (for example, in this situation you may be asked questions from the context of **learning**: how your hobbies impact on your studies, when you do homework etc.)

In the **presentation**, you may use notes consisting of five headings of no more than eight words in either English or Spanish, and/or you can use visual aids (such as drawings). These notes can help you with remembering key points or sentences but should not be read out as part of the presentation; they are for jogging your memory only.

Hints & tips

Remember to base your presentation on a topic that interests you or you know a lot about, choosing from the SQA list of contexts, topics and topic development. You will perform better if you talk about things that interest you or are important to you.

In the **conversation**, you will be asked questions by your teacher/lecturer, and you may ask some questions too. Remember, 5 of the 20 marks awarded for this section are for your ability to sustain the conversation (see marking instructions on p. 57). The type of information you provide in the conversation should be mainly of a factual nature with some ideas and opinions included.

Below are examples of presentations and conversations to help you prepare for the performance–talking.

The presentation

Your presentation should show your teacher/lecturer the range of language and grammatical structures you have learned. It is important to include a wide range of vocabulary and structures that display your knowledge. In addition to the content of the presentation, it is important to speak without undue hesitation, be confident and deliver the presentation with a good, steady voice. As you develop the skill of talking throughout the course, you should pay close attention to pronunciation and intonation to ensure your delivery of Spanish words are as good as they can be.

For practice

When you deliver a presentation, think about:

- **Your voice.** Is it strong? Do you sound confident? Do you pause slightly when you come to the end of a sentence?
- **Your speed.** Are you talking too quickly or too slowly? Develop a pace that is not too fast or slow.
- **Your delivery.** Are you pronouncing your words clearly?

Many of the aspects of delivering a presentation in English can be applied to your presentation in Spanish.

When preparing your presentation, break it down into three sections or paragraphs. This type of structure will help you remember the content more easily. Use the following example presentations for ideas on how to structure your presentation and the type of content to use.

Society: Family and relationships

This topic may be of interest to you as you can talk – if you wish – about your own family and friends. Remember to make it varied though and avoid simply describing everyone!

Section 1

Introduce the topic with a general statement about your relationship with your family and some information about them. Don't just list members of your family, as this won't allow you to show off a range of structures or detailed language.

Creo que en general mi familia y yo nos llevamos bastante bien. Somos cuatro, o sea, mis padres, mi hermano y yo. No es una familia grande pero es típica. Tengo que decir que mis padres son bastante comprensivos y a veces estrictos, pero es normal, ¿no? Sin embargo, mi hermano es otro caso – es muy molesto y aunque solo tiene doce años, cree que lo sabe todo. Y finalmente, ¡yo! Me dicen que soy paciente y amable pero debo confesar que de vez en cuando soy un poco gruñón.

This introduction uses a range of structures, such as *creo que...*, *tengo que decir que...* and *me dicen que...* . These help to elevate the level of language. It includes third-person singular verbs (the 'he/she' part of the verb): *es..., tiene..., cree..., sabe...* It includes a good range of adjectives (*comprensivos, estrictos, molesto, paciente, amable* and *gruñón*).

This introduction states who is in the speaker's family without simply listing them in order. There is also no physical detail here which tends to be too simplistic for National 5 level.

Section 2

Continue to explore the theme of relationships in your family.

Yo diría que, en general, me llevo bastante bien con mi familia aunque discutimos mucho por la música, la escuela y las tareas de casa. A veces, mi padre es muy estricto: cuando no hago nada en casa se enfada un poco. Mi hermano y yo no tenemos mucho en común, pero me gusta ayudarle con sus deberes, o si tiene un problema. Es verdad que mi madre y yo somos muy parecidos y compartimos los mismos intereses.

This section states some facts about the speaker's relationships, as well as adding some opinions. There is also a good range of different persons of the verb (e.g. *me llevo..., discutimos..., es..., tiene..., compartimos*).

Section 3

Explore other issues, such as housework, part-time jobs and/or going out.

Desafortunadamente, no puedo trabajar para ganar mi propio dinero porque mis padres dicen que soy demasiado joven. En vez de tener un trabajo a tiempo parcial, debo ayudar con las tareas de la casa: normalmente, suelo cargar el lavaplatos y pasar la aspiradora. Recibo veinte libras a la semana, y me gasto el dinero en ropa, música y salir con mis amigos. Me gustaría poder ganar y ahorrar dinero antes de ir a la universidad. Reconozco que no somos la familia perfecta, pero tengo que decir que no la cambiaría por nada del mundo.

Learning: Subject choice and future career plans

This topic is a good one to choose as it is perhaps easier to remember facts and opinions on what you are currently studying. However, you need to ensure that there is sufficient range of detailed language throughout the presentation and that it does not simply list subjects and your opinion of them.

Hints & tips

✓ Try to begin your presentation with an opinion of the topic.

✓ Use a wide range of vocabulary and structures in the opening section: this will set the tone for the rest of your presentation.

Section 1

Begin with some general statements about your school using a variety of introductory phrases. You may wish to describe the school, where it is and if there are any rules.

> Asisto a un instituto bastante grande, con unos mil alumnos y setenta profesores. Tengo suerte porque vivo cerca, así que puedo ir andando con mis amigos, tanto por la mañana como por la tarde. Llevamos un uniforme de color gris y rojo y a mi parecer el uniforme es importante para la seguridad. Sin embargo, no me permite expresar mi personalidad. Hay algunas reglas importantes en el instituto. Por ejemplo, se debe llegar a tiempo y no nos dejan fumar. La verdad es que no tengo problemas con las reglas del instituto.

There is evidence here of some good detailed language, such as *tengo suerte* and *tanto… como* which helps to lift the level of the introductory sentence. In addition, rather than listing all the rules of the school, two are selected here to highlight and comment on, bringing the opportunity to express an opinion.

Section 2

Move on to what you study and how you learn, and where your strengths (and weaknesses!) lie.

> Actualmente estoy en cuarto y he elegido estudiar dos ciencias (biología y física) y dos idiomas (español y francés). Es obligatorio estudiar inglés, mates y educación física. Quiero sacar buenas notas en todas mis asignaturas, así que debo estudiar la mayoría de las tardes. Disfruto de trabajar independientemente en clase pero claro, si no entiendo algo, mis profesores me ayudan. Diría que se me dan bien los idiomas y se me dan regular las ciencias.

The use of *es obligatorio estudiar* helps to avoid listing a long series of subjects and creates variety in sentence structure. Also, using a phrase such as *diría que* ('I would say that') is a good way to introduce your opinion or feeling about something.

Section 3

Outline what your studies can lead to. For example, talk about plans for future study at university or college, or about the type of career and job that your subjects could lead to.

> El curso que viene quiero seguir estudiando idiomas porque, después del instituto, me gustaría ir a la universidad. Me gustaría ser traductora o quizás trabajar en una empresa internacional. Quiero estudiar lejos de mi pueblo para tener más libertad y para ganar más experiencia.
>
> Lo tengo todo planeado – ¡ahora me hace falta estudiar mucho!

Hints & tips

✓ Don't simply list all of your subjects or what you like/dislike studying – try and use a variety of ways to describe what you study or what subjects you prefer.

✓ You can also use the 'we' person of the verb rather than 'I' all the time. For example: 'mis amigos y yo tenemos que estudiar mates e inglés porque son obligatorias'.

Employability: Work experience and future plans

This topic allows you to talk about any work experience you have had, such as part-time work, helping someone out in a job (for example, a family member who has their own business) or even babysitting. You could also discuss any formal work experience organised through your school/college. You can then relate your experience to any future career plans you may have.

This topic easily lends itself to using a good variety of tenses: discussing past work experience (preterite and imperfect tenses); talking about your skills and qualities (present tense); and outlining your career plans (conditional and future tenses). This progression through the tenses will also help with the structure of the presentation.

Section 1

Introduce the topic by discussing the skills and qualities you have which you think would be good for an employer. Giving other people's opinion of you also allows you to use other parts of the verb and shows a variety of vocabulary and language structures.

> Por regla general, creo que soy una persona bastante ambiciosa y me gusta aprender cosas nuevas. Mis amigos dicen que soy paciente, y que me interesa conocer a gente. Mis padres me consideran una persona madura y responsable, lo cual es fundamental para el mundo laboral. Me gusta trabajar en equipo y sé organizarme bien.

Section 2

Discuss any work experience you have had, and what benefits this has brought to you. This will be mainly written using past tenses, such as the preterite (what you did) and the imperfect (what the work experience was like).

> El año pasado, en noviembre, hice mis prácticas laborales en una oficina de abogados. Está situada en el centro de la ciudad y tuve que coger el tren. Pasé cinco días en la oficina y conocí a mucha gente nueva. Todo el mundo era muy amable y me ayudaba mucho. Hice una variedad de tareas, como archivar documentos, contestar el teléfono y hacer fotocopias.

Section 3

Talk about your future career plans, what types of job interest you and even where you would like to work.

> En el futuro, después del instituto, quiero tomarme un año sabático porque me gusta viajar. Quizás iré a Australia porque me parece un país interesante, además tengo familia que vive allí. También me gustaría estudiar derecho en la universidad porque me interesa ser abogada.

Culture: Holidays

A good way to organise a presentation on the topic of holidays it is to have an introductory section where you talk about what holidays mean to you and why they are important. You can then go on to talk about what you normally like to do on holiday and perhaps contrast this with a recent holiday (using the preterite). The third section can then talk about what your ideal holiday would be like (conditional tense).

Section 1

Use the first section to outline your general thoughts about holidays – what you like to do, where you go etc.

> Para mí las vacaciones son muy importantes porque es el momento perfecto para descansar y relajarme.
>
> Siempre paso las vacaciones de verano con mi familia: nos quedamos en una casa que alquilamos en el norte de Escocia. Está a unas tres horas de mi casa y viajamos en coche. Durante el viaje leo, escucho música o duermo un poco. El pueblo tiene playas preciosas y el agua está muy limpia pero un poco fría. Por la mañana, normalmente damos un paseo por la playa y después, comemos en uno de los restaurantes de la costa. Por la tarde, si hace sol, mi familia y yo jugamos en el jardín o si llueve, vemos una película.

As well as facts (where you normally go, how you travel there, what you do during the journey), include an opinion (why holidays are important to you).

Section 2

Contrast your normal holiday with a holiday you had in the past. This then allows you to introduce the preterite tense and use some verbs in this past form.

> El año pasado decidimos ir a Barcelona – en mi opinión, es una de las ciudades más bonitas del mundo. Fue la primera vez que viajé en avión, lo cual me gustó mucho. Mi familia y yo nos quedamos en un hotel justo en el centro. Era muy práctico porque el metro estaba muy cerca. El hotel era bastante grande con muchas instalaciones, como por ejemplo una piscina olímpica y dos gimnasios. Visitamos los monumentos turísticos pero debo confesar que mi lugar favorito fue el estadio 'Camp Nou' porque soy aficionado del Barça. Prefiero hacer cosas durante las vacaciones – no me gusta tumbarme en la playa y tomar el sol porque me quemo fácilmente.

Rather than listing lots of places you have visited on holiday, make your presentation more interesting by highlighting a favourite place you have visited. When describing where you stayed (as in the description of the hotel here) highlight the facilities that were important to you rather than writing a long list of what was there. Using reflexive verbs (here *tumbarme* and *me quemo*) is also a good way of showing more detailed language appropriate to National 5 level.

Hints & tips ⭐

Using a range of tenses throughout your presentation is another good way to show range of vocabulary. Some topics lend themselves naturally to present (what you normally do), past (what you did on one occasion) and future (what you will do) or conditional (what you would do). This type of structure also helps you to remember the content.

Section 3

Talk about what your ideal holiday would be like some time in the future. This then allows you to use your imagination!

> Aunque me encanta pasar las vacaciones con mi familia (normalmente nos llevamos genial), en el futuro, cuando sea más mayor, me gustaría ir de vacaciones con mis amigos. Creo que sería una buena experiencia. Siempre he soñado con visitar el sur de Francia. Hablo un poco de francés y la abuela de uno de mis amigos tiene una casa cerca de Niza. Como soy aventurero, sería ideal viajar en barco y luego en tren – para mí, viajar de esta forma resultaría más emocionante.
>
> Francamente, me encanta viajar porque puedo conocer a gente interesante y lugares sorprendentes, y aprender muchas cosas nuevas.

Conversation

In the conversation section of the performance–talking, your teacher/ lecturer will ask you some follow-up questions related to the topic/ context of your presentation. They will then ask you questions on one of the other contexts. Your teacher/lecturer will know in advance the two contexts you choose to discuss in the conversation.

It is important to remember it is a conversation, and you should answer the questions carefully, using a range of detailed language. The conversation should last for approximately 5–6 minutes, and during this time you may also ask your teacher/lecturer some questions.

The skill of responding in a conversation in Spanish is one that you will develop throughout the National 5 Spanish course. You should ensure you are practising in class as well as at home. Your teacher/lecturer must use the marking Instructions (provided on pp. 55–57) to assess you. It is important therefore to ensure your answers are full and contain enough detail for your teacher/lecturer to be able to assess you appropriately.

You will have time in class and at home to prepare material on your two chosen contexts and topics. This should then allow you to draw on material and develop this in your answers.

Remember – when answering a question, extend it rather than waiting for a follow-up question from your teacher/lecturer. For example, look again at the example presentation given above for the Context: Society, Topic: Family and relationships. As a follow-up question to this presentation, the teacher/lecturer might ask: *¿Y tienes muchos amigos?* ('Do you have many friends?') This is a closed question, and you could answer with *sí* or *no*! However, there would be very little content on which to assess your ability to use detailed language in Spanish. Therefore, it would be better to answer with something along the lines of:

Hints & tips ★

In order to practise Spanish conversation at home, try the following:

✓ *Write questions on different cards. Turn them over one at a time and answer out loud in Spanish.*

✓ *Record yourself at home talking about your topic. Time yourself too – what can you say in 20 seconds? 40 seconds? 60 seconds?*

Pues la verdad es que sí, tengo muchos amigos. Sin embargo, mi mejor amigo se llama James. Creo que es muy leal y somos muy parecidos. Tenemos mucho en común, como por ejemplo la música y las asignaturas.

This ending will also lead naturally into your teacher/lecturer asking a question around your subjects, musical tastes, or your interests, and you can be prepared for that.

Hints & tips ⭐

The best way to structure an answer is to make sure you include:

✓ a range of opinion phrases (see Chapter 8)
✓ a beginning, a middle and an ending
✓ additional information that is relevant
✓ filler words such as 'pues...', 'bien...' etc. – this also gives you some thinking time

Below is a series of questions on the topic of holidays, with some suggested ways you may wish to respond.

¿Dónde sueles pasar las vacaciones de verano?	Talk about where you usually go on holiday – give details such as who with, what type of places they are. Include an opinion phrase (i.e. what you think of the places you mentioned). For example:
	En general, suelo pasar las vacaciones de verano en el extranjero, en particular en España o en Italia. A mis padres les gusta el calor, y estos países tienen muy buen clima. Siempre voy con mi familia y nos llevamos bien durante las vacaciones. Desde mi perspectiva, ir a España e Italia me da la oportunidad de aprender otras culturas y probar otro tipo de comida.
¿Con quién pasas las vacaciones?	This could be a basic question, but by using contrast/compare type phrases you can show a range of vocabulary. For example:
	Normalmente, paso las vacaciones con mi familia (mis padres y mi hermano mayor) porque solo tengo dieciséis años. Sin embargo, en el futuro, me gustaría visitar los Estados Unidos con mis amigos porque creo que sería una muy buena experiencia.
¿Dónde te alojas?	To make this more interesting and more detailed, include what sort of facilities the accommodation you stay in has. For example:
	Por regla general, nos alojamos en un hotel con muchas instalaciones, como por ejemplo una piscina, gimnasios y buenos restaurantes. Prefiero los hoteles que están situados cerca de la playa porque me gusta ver el agua y la arena.
¿Te gusta ir de vacaciones con tus padres?	Begin with a general statement and then give some detail.
	En general, sí me gusta estar con mi familia pero a veces mis padres no me dan mucha libertad. Y no me gusta visitar museos – ¡en mi opinión son aburridos!
¿Adónde fuiste de vacaciones el año pasado?	To make this answer more detailed, add in some opinion phrases and some contrast.
	En julio mi madre, mi hermano y yo fuimos al sur de Escocia y nos quedamos en un camping. Era muy divertido porque había muchos jóvenes de mi edad. Sin embargo, ¡hizo frío por la noche!
¿Cómo serían tus vacaciones ideales?	This question requires you to use the conditional tense in your answer. You can also expand it by adding in what types of activities you would do.
	La verdad es que mis vacaciones ideales serían con mi mejor amigo e iríamos a España. Nos gustaría visitar Barcelona porque a los dos nos gustan las grandes ciudades. Nos quedaríamos en un gran hotel de lujo.

En tu opinión, ¿por qué hay tanta gente que va a España a pasar las vacaciones?	This question is asking for your opinion. Add an explanation for your thinking.
	Desde mi punto de vista, la gente visita España por el clima (hace mucho calor), está bastante cerca de Escocia y tiene mucho que ofrecer. También, creo que la gente es muy simpática.
¿Adónde irás de vacaciones este verano?	You can use both forms of the future tense here: what you are going to do and what you will do. This will show your teacher/lecturer a variety and range of language structures.
	Pues, este verano mi madre quiere ir al norte de Escocia porque es muy aventurera. Vamos a pasar una semana haciendo mucho deporte, como por ejemplo la vela, el montañismo y nadar en los lagos. Nos quedaremos en un albergue juvenil y seguro que conoceré a mucha gente nueva.

Presentation			
Content	Accuracy	Language resource	Pegged marks
The candidate: • uses content which is relevant and well-organised • expresses a wide range of ideas and opinions • speaks without undue hesitation	The candidate: • demonstrates a very good degree of grammatical accuracy corresponding to the level, although may make a few errors which do not detract from the overall impression • uses pronunciation and intonation which are sufficient to be readily understood by a speaker of the language	The candidate: • uses **detailed** language throughout • uses a wide range of structures • uses a wide range of verbs/verb forms, tenses (if appropriate) and other language features	10
The candidate: • uses content which is mostly relevant and well-organised • expresses a range of ideas and opinions • may speak with occasional hesitation but recovers successfully	The candidate: • demonstrates a good degree of grammatical accuracy corresponding to the level. Errors may occasionally detract from the overall impression • uses pronunciation and intonation which are sufficient to be understood by a speaker of the language	The candidate: • mostly uses **detailed** language • uses a range of structures • uses a range of verbs/verb forms, tenses (if appropriate) and other language features	8
The candidate: • uses content which is generally relevant and well-organised • expresses some ideas and opinions • hesitates on a few occasions, but attempts to recover	The candidate: • demonstrates an adequate degree of grammatical accuracy corresponding to the level, although errors detract from the overall impression • uses pronunciation and intonation which are sufficient to be understood by a speaker of the language, although some points may not be immediately clear	The candidate: • attempts to use **detailed** language • attempts to use a range of structures • uses a few different verbs/verb forms, tenses (if appropriate) and other language features	6

Conversation			
Content	Accuracy	Language resource	Pegged marks
The candidate: • uses content which is relevant and well-organised • expresses a wide range of ideas and opinions • covers a different context to that used in the presentation	The candidate: • demonstrates a very good degree of grammatical accuracy corresponding to the level, although may make a few errors which do not detract from the overall impression • uses pronunciation and intonation which are sufficient to be readily understood by a speaker of the language	The candidate: • responds using a wide range of **detailed** language • responds using a wide range of structures • responds using a wide range of verbs/verb forms, tenses (if appropriate) and other language features	15
The candidate: • uses content which is mostly relevant and well-organised • expresses a range of ideas and opinions • covers a different context to that used in the presentation	The candidate: • demonstrates a good degree of grammatical accuracy corresponding to the level. Errors may occasionally detract from the overall impression • uses pronunciation and intonation which are sufficient to be understood by a speaker of the language	The candidate: • responds using a range of **detailed** language • responds using a range of structures • responds using a range of verbs/verb forms, tenses (if appropriate) and other language features	12
The candidate: • uses content which is generally relevant and well-organised • expresses some ideas and opinions • may not cover a different context to that used in the presentation	The candidate: • demonstrates an adequate degree of grammatical accuracy corresponding to the level, although errors detract from the overall impression • uses pronunciation and intonation which are sufficient to be understood by a speaker of the language, although some points may not be immediately clear	The candidate: • attempts to respond using **detailed** language • attempts to respond using a range of structures • responds using a few different verbs/verb forms, tenses (if appropriate) and other language features	9

Conversation — natural element	
The candidate readily sustains the conversation, for example:	Pegged mark
• understands almost all of what is said	5
• speaks without undue hesitation or recovers successfully when there is such hesitation	
• deals with unpredictable elements	
• may occasionally seek clarification in the modern language	
• may take the initiative (e.g. ask relevant questions and/or expand on an answer)	
• may use some interjections and/or connectives	
The candidate adequately sustains the conversation, for example:	Pegged mark
• understands most of what is said	3
• hesitates occasionally, affecting the flow of the conversation	
• mostly deals with unpredictable elements	
• may attempt to seek clarification in the modern language, but not always successfully	
• may occasionally take the initiative	
• may attempt to use some interjections and/or connectives, but not always successfully	
• may require some support and/or prompting from the interlocutor	
The candidate has difficulty in sustaining the conversation, for example:	Pegged mark
• understands only some of what is said	1
• hesitates in most responses	
• has difficulty dealing with most unpredictable elements	
• requires support and/or prompting from the interlocutor	
• may attempt to seek clarification in the modern language, but often unsuccessfully	
The candidate cannot sustain the conversation, for example:	Pegged mark
• understands little of what is said	0
• is unable to seek clarification in the modern language or does so ineffectively	
• hesitates throughout	
• is unable to deal with unpredictable elements	
• requires significant support and/or prompting from the interlocutor	

Chapter 6

Writing: the final exam

In the final writing exam, you are asked to write an e-mail in Spanish in response to a job advert. Every year the advert is different, but it always provides details of what type of job (for example, shop assistant, receptionist) and other details such as what the job is or where it is situated.

The writing question paper is given to you at the same time as the reading question paper and you will have 1 hour and 30 minutes in which to complete both. Therefore, it is important that you practise timing as well as content for both papers. You should take approximately 30 minutes for the writing question. This will allow you to plan it, write it and check it over.

The task will be based on a scenario given in English, along with a job advert in Spanish. You will be required to provide specified information in a piece of writing of 120–150 words. You are allowed to use a dictionary.

The scenario always involves you writing to apply for a job or a work experience placement, in the form of an e-mail. The scenario is always given with six bullet points that you have to cover. The first four bullet points are the same every time; the last two change from year to year. The first four bullet points ask you to write:

- personal details (name, age, where you live)
- school/college/education experience until now
- skills/interests you have which make you right for the job
- related work experience

The two additional bullet points are 'unpredictable' points. This chapter will help you prepare for them, showing you how to 'manipulate' language you know to answer correctly and accurately.

To help you prepare for this writing exam, you can source material from your class textbooks and notes, as well as work you produce throughout the National 5 Spanish course. This allows you to plan what you will write on the day of exam, and just as importantly, undertake regular practice.

See Chapter 8 for suggested phrases and sentences to use in your writing exam which will enable you to access higher marks.

> ### Hints & tips ⭐
>
> *Aim for 20–30 words per bullet. This allows you to write more for one or two of them. It also means you know how many words you are using, and you don't need to waste time counting them.*

> ### Hints & tips ⭐
>
> ✓ *Write your e-mail in clear, distinct paragraphs – use a different paragraph for each bullet point. This makes it clear for you when checking, and also clear for the marker when marking.*
> ✓ *Use a range of tenses/persons throughout your writing and make sure they are accurate.*
> ✓ *Use a wide range of vocabulary.*
> ✓ *Use conjunctions to make longer, more detailed sentences as appropriate to the level.*

Keep the following advice in mind when you approach this task:
- Read the job advert – make sure your e-mail is relevant.
- Tick off the bullet points as you complete each one.
- Use your time wisely – make sure you have a couple of minutes left over at the end to check accuracy.
- Be prepared – have the first four bullet points learned and be ready for the last two bullet points by practising several examples in class and when you revise at home.
- Write in the order of the bullets.

Practice

You can use the last two bullet points from SQA past papers (Spanish and the other modern languages) to practise how you would respond in Spanish. Practising these regularly will help you to:
- develop an awareness of the vocabulary areas that come up
- check your accuracy: spelling, accents, verb endings

Example response to a job advert

The following is an example of a job advert and suggested ways to address each of the bullet points.

Questions

You are preparing an application for the job advertised below. Write an e-mail in **Spanish** to the company.

Empresa multinacional "Los almacenes Almudena" busca jóvenes para trabajar en su oficina en el centro de Madrid durante los meses de julio y agosto. Se necesita un buen nivel de español.

To help you to write your e-mail, you have been given the following checklist. You must include all of these points:

- personal details (name, age, where you live)
- school/college/education experience until now
- skills/interests you have which make you right for the job
- related work experience
- why you would like to work in Spain
- when you can start the job

Use all of the above to help you write the e-mail in **Spanish**. The e-mail should be approximately 120–150 words. You may use a Spanish dictionary.

The first four bullet points are the same every year, so make use of the time throughout your course to develop strong, accurate responses to these that will show the marker your accuracy, content and wide range of vocabulary and language structures, including verbs, tenses and conjunctions.

Bullet point 1: personal details (name, age, where you live)

Make sure the information you give is clear and comprehensive.

> **Primero, me voy a presentar: me llamo Andrew Roberts, tengo dieciséis años y en este momento vivo en el centro de Glasgow en Escocia.** (24 words)

Bullet point 2: school/college/education experience until now

Give details of what you are studying but avoid simply listing them (this is too basic). In this example, the advert specifies a requirement for knowledge of Spanish, and gives a natural opportunity to state what you study.

> **Actualmente soy alumno de instituto. Tenemos una selección de asignaturas obligatorias y optativas: tenemos que estudiar inglés y mates, y, este curso, yo he elegido estudiar español y ciencias.** (29 words)

Bullet point 3: skills/interests you have which make you right for the job

Describe general characteristics that make you employable. Add detail relevant to the job being advertised.

> **Mis profesores dicen que soy responsable y que aprendo fácilmente. Tengo un buen nivel de conocimientos de informática y me interesa conocer a gente nueva.** (25 words)

Bullet point 4: related work experience

Write about any relevant work experience you have had and your skills. This can be formal work experience organised by your school/college, part-time jobs, voluntary work or any work tasks you have done. Use the preterite tense when writing about past work experience. Make the 'related' part relevant by including information about, for example, working with customers or writing about your communication skills as these will generally cover most of the jobs in the task.

> **Durante mis prácticas laborales trabajé en una clínica veterinaria durante una semana. Aprendí mucho sobre el mundo laboral. Soy una persona sociable y me gusta trabajar en equipo. Además, tengo buenas destrezas comunicativas.** (33 words)

Bullet points 5 and 6

The last two bullet points change each year, and might be related to the specific job advertised or be more generic. If you write approximately 100 words for the first four bullet points then you have approximately 20 words left for each of the last two bullet points.

The following is a selection of sample bullet points to give you an idea on the type of areas they cover:

- why you would like to work in Spain
- what you hope to get from the experience of working in Spain

- requesting further information about the job
- experiences you have of working or living abroad
- reasons for applying for the job
- your availability for interview or for starting the job
- which languages you speak
- what your strengths are

The sample scenario here is for a job in the office for a chain of large department stores. Bullet point 5 asks why you would like to work in Spain, so you could give two reasons.

Me gustaría trabajar en España porque quiero aprender más sobre la cultura y tener experiencia de vivir en otro país. (20 words)

Hints & tips ⭐

By giving two reasons you can use two different infinitives, e.g. 'aprender' and 'tener'.

Try to keep it concise but accurate! For things you would like to do, you can also use phrases such as *quisiera, me interesaría* or *me resultaría interesante*.

The last bullet point asks when you can start the job. You can address this directly by saying 'I can start the job on…' and give a specific date. You can use *puedo* for 'I can' or you could use another tense such as the future *podré* for 'I will be able' or the conditional *podría* for 'I would be able'.

Podré empezar el puesto a partir del 28 de junio después de mis exámenes escolares. (15 words)

The marking categories for writing are as follows:

Hints & tips ⭐

✓ *Keep bullet points 5 and 6 concise. Practise how you address them by looking at past papers on the SQA website, not just in Spanish but in the other modern languages — you will have a wide range of bullet points to practise with.*

✓ *Always leave time in the exam to check accuracy.*

Category	Mark	Content	Accuracy	Language resource – variety, range, structures
Very good	20	The job advert has been addressed in a full and balanced way. The candidate uses detailed language. The candidate addresses the advert completely and competently, including **information in response to both unpredictable bullet points**. A range of verbs/verb forms, tenses and constructions is used. Overall this comes over as a competent, well thought-out and serious application for the job.	The candidate handles all aspects of grammar and spelling accurately, although the language may contain one or two minor errors. Where the candidate attempts to use language more appropriate to Higher, a slightly higher number of inaccuracies need not detract from the overall very good impression.	The candidate is comfortable with the first person of the verb and generally uses a different verb in each sentence. Some modal verbs and infinitives may be used. There is good use of adjectives, adverbs and prepositional phrases and, where appropriate, word order. There may be a range of tenses. The candidate uses co-ordinating conjunctions and/or subordinate clauses where appropriate. The language of the e-mail flows well.

Category	Mark	Content	Accuracy	Language resource – variety, range, structures
Good	16	The job advert has been addressed competently. There is less evidence of detailed language. The candidate uses a reasonable range of verbs/verb forms. Overall, the candidate has produced a genuine, reasonably accurate attempt at applying for the specific job, even though he/she **may not address one of the unpredictable bullet points**.	The candidate handles a range of verbs fairly accurately. There are some errors in spelling, adjective endings and, where relevant, case endings. Use of accents is less secure, where appropriate. Where the candidate is attempting to use more complex vocabulary and structures, these may be less successful, although basic structures are used accurately. There may be one or two examples of inaccurate dictionary use, especially in the unpredictable bullet points.	There may be repetition of verbs. There may be examples of listing, in particular when referring to school/college experience, without further amplification. There may be one or two examples of a co-ordinating conjunction, but most sentences are simple sentences. The candidate keeps to more basic vocabulary, particularly in response to either or both unpredictable bullet points.
Satisfactory	12	The job advert has been addressed fairly competently. The candidate makes limited use of detailed language. The language is fairly repetitive and uses a limited range of verbs and fixed phrases, e.g. *I like, I go, I play*. The candidate copes fairly well with areas of personal details, education, skills, interests and work experience but does not deal fully with the two unpredictable bullet points and indeed **may not address either or both of the unpredictable bullet points**. On balance, however, the candidate has produced a satisfactory job application in the specific language.	The verbs are generally correct, but may be repetitive. There are quite a few errors in other parts of speech – gender of nouns, cases, singular/plural confusion, for instance. Prepositions may be missing, e.g. *I go the town*. Overall, there is more correct than incorrect.	The candidate copes with the first and third person of a few verbs, where appropriate. A limited range of verbs is used. Sentences are basic and mainly brief. There is minimal use of adjectives, probably mainly after is, e.g. *Chemistry is interesting*. The candidate has a weak knowledge of plurals. There may be several spelling errors, e.g. reversal of vowel combinations.
Unsatisfactory	8	The job advert has been addressed in an uneven manner and/or with insufficient use of detailed language. The language is repetitive, e.g. *I like, I go, I play* may feature several times. There may be little difference between Satisfactory and Unsatisfactory. **Either or both of the unpredictable bullet points may not have been addressed.** There may be one sentence which is not intelligible to a sympathetic native speaker.	Ability to form tenses is inconsistent. There are errors in many other parts of speech – gender of nouns, cases, singular/plural confusion, for instance. Several errors are serious, perhaps showing mother tongue interference. The detail in the unpredictable bullet points may be very weak. Overall, there is more incorrect than correct.	The candidate copes mainly only with the personal language required in bullet points 1 and 2. The verbs *is* and *study* may also be used correctly. Sentences are basic. An English word may appear in the writing. There may be an example of serious dictionary misuse.

Category	Mark	Content	Accuracy	Language resource – variety, range, structures
Poor	4	The candidate has had considerable difficulty in addressing the job advert. There is little evidence of the use of detailed language. Three or four sentences may not be understood by a sympathetic native speaker. **Either or both of the unpredictable bullet points may not have been addressed.**	Many of the verbs are incorrect. There are many errors in other parts of speech – personal pronouns, gender of nouns, cases, singular/plural confusion, for instance. The language is probably inaccurate throughout the writing.	The candidate cannot cope with more than one or two basic verbs. The candidate displays almost no knowledge of the present tense of verbs. Verbs used more than once may be written differently on each occasion. Sentences are very short. The candidate has a very limited vocabulary. Several English words may appear in the writing. There are examples of serious dictionary misuse.
Very poor	0	The candidate is unable to address the job advert. The two unpredictable bullet points may not have been addressed. Very little is intelligible to a sympathetic native speaker.	Virtually nothing is correct.	The candidate may only cope with the verbs *to have* and *to be*. Very few words are written correctly in the modern language. English words are used. There may be several examples of mother tongue interference. There may be several examples of dictionary misuse.

Chapter 7

Writing: the assignment

For this part of the National 5 Spanish course, you will produce a piece of writing in Spanish in class and, once re-drafted in class, the final version will be sent to SQA for marking.

There are 20 marks available in this part of the exam (scaled to 15), and your writing should show that you can use detailed Spanish language accurately. You should express a range of ideas and opinions and use content which is relevant. Your writing should show variation in structures, tenses and vocabulary.

For the assignment you will write 120–200 words in Spanish on a topic from the contexts of **society**, **learning** or **culture** (the context of **employability** is in the writing paper where you write an e-mail in response to a job advert). Your topic should be something that interests you so that you can write sufficient content for it. Although your topic is based on one of the three contexts, you can of course use content from other contexts that is relevant. For example, you may choose to write about your views on your school and you could include content on what you do outside of school to get a good school–life balance.

You teacher/lecturer can give you some examples of topics to choose from (these will be either ones from SQA or ones they have created themselves). These will be a series of bullet points in English to help you as a stimulus for your ideas. You can also discuss with your teacher/lecturer any topics or ideas you want to write about. Importantly, you won't see the actual bullet points until you are ready to write the first draft of your assignment.

The four stages

There are four stages to writing your assignment:

Stage 1

When you and your teacher/lecturer feel that you are ready to undertake the assignment, you will choose a context as the focus of your writing and your teacher/lecturer will give you a series of bullet points in English (usually three or four) to help you as a stimulus for the piece of writing.

You will then write about these in Spanish and produce a first draft of your assignment. You will have access to several resources at the point of writing, including:

- a bilingual dictionary
- grammar notes and verb tables
- any vocabulary lists you have relevant to the topic chosen
- the writing stimulus (the bullet points)

You then produce your first draft in class, which you give to your teacher/lecturer.

Hints & tips ⭐

✓ *You cannot use textbooks or reading texts in Spanish (either in paper format or online) nor can you make use of any web-based resources.*

✓ *You cannot use any lists of phrases or expressions nor can you have access to any writing scaffolding or writing frames.*

Stage 2

Your teacher/lecturer will give you feedback and will comment on your first draft. They will provide annotations to help you identify anything that you need to look at again or correct. They won't correct your work – that is for you to do using their annotations.

You will be given time to reflect on your first draft and think about the areas you need to revise/correct. Although you will not be able to take the draft home, you should use time at home to revise any areas that you need to work on. For example, it may be that your use of the present tense is inaccurate in a number of places, so you would spend time in class and at home revising and practising the present tense in order to develop more confidence and familiarity with conjugating verbs in the present tense when you go back to work on your final version.

Stage 3

In class, you will write a final version of your assignment. You can use the same resources listed above as well as your first draft with annotations.

Stage 4

You write your final version in the SQA answer booklet. When you have finished, you hand both the final version and the draft version back to your teacher/lecturer. On the final version, you must include the context you have chosen and the title of your piece (for example. **Context: Society; Title: My family and me**).

Preparation for the writing assignment

Throughout your study for National 5 Spanish, you will undertake work in class and at home to help you develop your writing skills in Spanish. This could be learning about grammar, developing your knowledge of the vocabulary areas associated with the three contexts and practise tasks to help you build the skills you will need.

Hints & tips ⭐

✓ *Any practice you do for talking preparation or the job e-mail writing is also practice for developing your skills for writing the assignment.*

✓ *This includes how you structure your writing for these areas, and the range of grammar and vocabulary that you use.*

Your assignment should be based on mainly facts about the topic, and you should write in paragraphs and have a structure to the writing (an introduction, a development of facts and ideas, and then a short conclusion). Look at the example of a writing assignment below to see how you do this. You should:

- Include ideas and opinions that are relevant to the topic and the bullet points.
- Use a good range of expressions and structures (see Chapter 8).
- If you are expressing an opinion on something, remember to give a reason for this. For example:

Me encanta ser alumno en mi instituto porque en general los profesores son muy buenos y me ayudan mucho con mis estudios.

Hints & tips ⭐

Checking your work

It is important to develop the skill of checking your writing for accuracy (correct spelling, accurate grammar usage etc.). Learning vocabulary correctly and practising grammar will help with accuracy in your writing. You will not have time in the writing-up of the assignment to check every word in the dictionary, so it is better to learn vocabulary and grammar throughout the course.

When preparing for the assignment, remember that the marks awarded will be based on three main areas: the content of your assignment (facts, ideas, opinions and reasons all relevant to the context and the title), the level of accuracy and the variety of vocabulary and language structures. In particular, the markers are looking at:

- your use of detailed Spanish language
- the organisation and structure of your writing
- the range of vocabulary and language structures
- the range of language features and tenses (where appropriate)

It is important to have a range of language features with a high level of accuracy to access marks of 16 or 20. For these marks, you need to use more complex language (including structures and opinion expressions) as well as a range of verb tenses (and persons of the verb). By doing this, you will show the SQA marker a high degree of control across the three main areas.

The table below shows what is expected of you for a mark of 12, 16 or 20.

Content	Accuracy	Language resource	Pegged Marks
The candidate: • addresses the title in a full and balanced way • uses content which is relevant • expresses a wide range of ideas, opinions and reasons • writes in a very structured and organised way and the language flows well	The candidate: • demonstrates a very good degree of grammatical accuracy corresponding to the level, although may make a few errors which do not detract from the overall impression • demonstrates a very good degree of accuracy in spelling and, where appropriate, word order	The candidate: • uses **detailed** language throughout • uses a wide range of structures • uses a wide range of verbs/verb forms, tenses (if appropriate) and other language features	20
The candidate: • addresses the title competently • uses content which is mostly relevant • expresses a range of ideas, opinions and reasons • writes in a structured and organised way	The candidate: • demonstrates a good degree of grammatical accuracy corresponding to the level; errors may occasionally detract from the overall impression • demonstrates a good degree of accuracy in spelling and, where appropriate, word order	The candidate: • mostly uses **detailed** language • uses a range of structures • uses a range of verbs/verb forms, tenses (if appropriate) and other language features • may occasionally repeat structures, verbs, etc.	16
The candidate: • addresses the title fairly competently • uses content which is generally relevant • expresses some ideas, opinions and reasons • writes with an adequate sense of structure and writing is mostly organised	The candidate: • demonstrates an adequate degree of grammatical accuracy corresponding to the level, although errors, which occasionally may be serious, detract from the overall impression • demonstrates an adequate degree of accuracy in spelling and, where appropriate, word order • produces more correct language than incorrect	The candidate: • attempts to use **detailed** language • attempts to use a range of structures • uses a few different verbs/verb forms, tenses (if appropriate) and other language features • may use fairly repetitive language • may use some lists	12

Hints & tips ⭐

✓ *Don't translate from English to Spanish! Instead, use expressions and structures you have learned and used in class.*

✓ *Think about the structure of your writing. Plan a short opening sentence or two, then three or four paragraphs on each of the suggested bullet points.*

✓ *Use a variety of opinion phrases and structures (see Chapter 8) — these are a good way of ensuring you use a wide range of vocabulary.*

✓ *Give reasons for your opinions — if you are stating what you think or believe, follow it up with a reason why.*

✓ *Use a logical structure and write about something you are interested in. Both will help you to remember the assignment when it comes to stages 1 and 3.*

✓ *As for the advice for planning your job e-mail (Chapter 7), and for your presentation and conversation (Chapter 6), try to avoid just giving lists of words as these will not show more detailed language. Instead, give examples and expand on these.*

✓ *Use your bilingual dictionary to check anything you are not sure of (but only use it to check a few words or you will lose time).*

Remember that for stage 3 of your writing you will have had your feedback from your teacher/lecturer and you will have had time to reflect and go over any areas you need to. You will also have the annotated first draft to refer to, and can make use of the resources listed on p. 64.

There is no set time for undertaking the first draft or the final stage of your writing, but you must remember that you cannot take either away with you – they have to remain with your teacher. That is why you will only do the assignment (all stages) when both you and your teacher/lecturer believe you are ready to do so.

Hints & tips

✓ To use other persons of the verb – introduce the opinion or experience of someone else/other people.

✓ To use other verb tenses – introduce a contrast. For example, if you are writing about something you do or like now, contrast this with what you used to do/like or what you would do/like etc.

Example of a writing assignment

SQA has published suggestions for possible writing topics. The following example gives an idea of how to structure and lay out the writing assignment.

Society: Sports and attitudes to sport

Write 120–200 words in Spanish.

You write an article about sport and health, in Spanish, for your online school magazine.

You could include the following:

- what sports you like to do and why
- sports facilities available in your school and local community
- your views on the importance of sport for a healthy lifestyle
- what other activities are important for a healthy lifestyle

The first thing to consider is which bullet points you want to address in your writing. For example, if you choose all four of the bullet points above, you could write approximately 40 words on each which would give you about 160 words in total.

Hints & tips ★

✓ *Stick to the required length of 120–200 words.*

✓ *If you make it too short, your content may be insufficient or you may not be able to show a range of vocabulary and language structures.*

✓ *If you make it too long, you may make more errors in accuracy.*

When checking if you have enough content, think 'Have I written enough to address the topic and to show the marker what I can do?'

Introduction

To start off your assignment, use an introductory statement, for example:

Desde mi perspectiva, el deporte es esencial para llevar una vida sana. Creo que el deporte es bueno tanto para la salud física como mental. (25 words)

Bullet point 1: what sports you like and why

Write about the types of sports you do, when you do them, who with and where. Choose one or two sports rather than just giving a list – this means you can expand and give some detail. Also, make good use of a range of opinion phrases and reasons when you explain why you do certain sports or sporting activities.

A mí me encantan los deportes de equipo. Todos los miércoles por la tarde mis amigos y yo jugamos al baloncesto en el parque. ¡Nos lo pasamos genial! Suelo jugar al fútbol durante el recreo, y es una buena manera de olvidar el estrés de las clases. (47 words)

Bullet point 2: sports facilities available in your school and local community

Make sure you choose a couple of examples and give your opinion of them.

Tengo suerte porque hay un polideportivo en mi pueblo. No es muy grande, pero tiene una variedad de instalaciones deportivas, como por ejemplo, una piscina olímpica y un gimnasio bien equipado. (31 words)

Bullet points 3: your views on the importance of sport for a healthy lifestyle

Include some other tenses to show variation in the verbs. For example, to write about your views on the importance of sport for a healthy lifestyle, show a contrast between what you used to think or do with what you think or do now.

Cuando era más joven, pensaba que el deporte no era necesario. Sin embargo, ahora me doy cuenta de que un poco de ejercicio me mantiene sano y me relaja. En mi opinión, lo importante es intentar hacer un poco ejercicio por lo menos tres veces a la semana. (48 words)

Bullet point 4: what other activities are important for a healthy lifestyle

Write about things you have to do to have a healthy lifestyle, such as eating a balanced diet and taking time to talk to others if you have a problem. You could also write about what you should avoid doing, such as smoking or eating too much fatty food.

> **También es necesario comer sano: intento tomar fruta todos los días y no comer mucho chocolate. Y por supuesto, si tengo un problema, mis amigos me ayudan y me apoyan.** (30 words)

Conclusion

When you have finished addressing the bullet points, add a short conclusion. For example, for this topic you could say:

> **En resumen, hace falta tener el deporte en tu vida porque, desde mi punto de vista, te ayuda a controlar mejor el estrés.** (23 words)

Annotation codes

When your teacher/lecturer gives to you back the first draft of your assignment you will see some annotations teacher/lecturer may have used to indicate errors. These will indicate what you need to work on when you write the final version of the assignment. The table below shows examples of annotation codes that your teacher/lecturer could use on your first draft.

Code	Meaning
^	omission/something missing
aa	adjectival agreement/problem with agreement of the adjective(s)
ap	adjectival position/problem with position of adjective(s)
acc	accent missing
dict	dictionary/wrong word
ew	extra word/words not required
g	gender
gr	grammar problem/incorrect grammar
np	new paragraph
ns	new sentence
mv	missing verb
mw	missing word
punct	punctuation
prep	preposition to check
rep	repetition
s? (<u>text underlined</u>)	not making sense
struct	structure – incorrect or does not exist
sg/pl	singular/plural
sp	spelling
t	tense
ve	verb ending
vt	wrong verb tense
wo	word order
ww	wrong word

Hints & tips ⭐

Remember that the assignment will always remain in the classroom.

✓ *If you have verb errors, use verb tables to help you make corrections as verb forms will not be in the dictionary.*

✓ *If something you have written does not make sense, it is possibly because you have translated directly from English to Spanish and this often does not work. That is why it is important to do language practice in class and at home and to learn your vocabulary and grammar.*

Opinions and grammatical structures

Using opinion phrases, conjunctions and a range of grammatical structures – including parts of the verb, a range of verb tenses, conjunctions (words and phrases that connect ideas in a sentence) and opinion phrases – will help you to access higher marks in your writing and talking.

Opinions

In the chapters covering the writing tasks (both the assignment and the job e-mail) and in the talking task (presentation and conversation) chapters, there are examples of structures you can use, which include a range of opinion phrases, such as those listed below. Using a variety of these in your writing and talking will help you to access higher marks – provided you use them appropriately, and the rest of your language is accurate, of course. Use the phrases to introduce something you think or feel, or something someone else thinks or feels.

Key words

Desde mi punto de vista...	From my point of view...
Desde mi perspectiva...	From my perspective...
Desde su punto de vista...	From his/her point of view...
En mi opinión...	In my opinion...
En la opinión de mi hermano...	In my brother's opinion...
Creo que...	I believe that...
Mis amigos y yo creemos que...	My friends and I believe that...
Pienso que...	I think that...
Tengo la opinión de que...	I have the opinion that...
A mi ver...	As I see it...
A mi parecer...	As I understand it...
Si me preguntas...	If you ask me...
En lo que se refiere a mí...	As far as I'm concerned...
Me resulta importante...	It's important to me...
Me parece ridículo...	It seems ridiculous to me...
Me gustaría...	I would like to...
Hace falta pensar que...	It's necessary to think that...
(No) Se debe...	One must (mustn't)...
(No) Se debería...	One should (shouldn't)...

Here are two examples of sentences expressing opinions:

A mi ver, comer bien es fundamental para la buena salud física.	As I see it, eating well is crucial for good physical health.
Me resulta importante tener un equilibrio en la vida.	It's important for me to have balance in my life.

Using conjunctions

Conjunctions are the words and phrases that you can use to join two ideas (or more) in a sentence, and they will help make your language more detailed (see table below). This is important in both your writing (job e-mail and the assignment) and talking (presentation and conversation). You should ensure you have a good range of opinions and conjunctions in your talking preparation, and throughout your writing assignment. When you give an opinion on something, it is a good idea to say why, so use a conjunction to connect your opinion and the reason(s) together.

Key words

y	and
pero	but
porque	because
sin embargo/no obstante	however
primero/segundo/tercero	firstly/secondly/thirdly
finalmente	finally
por regla general	in general
de vez en cuando	from time to time
además	besides/in addition
también	also/too
mientras	while
cuando	when

Here are two examples in which conjunctions are used to join two ideas together:

*Me llevo muy bien con mi familia porque estamos muy unidos. **Sin embargo**, también tenemos problemas de vez en cuando.*	I got on well with my family because we are very close. However, there are problems too from time to time.
*Por regla general, uso mi móvil para chatear en las redes sociales con mis amigos. **Además**, lo uso para hacer mis deberes en línea.*	In general, I use my mobile to chat on social media with my friends. In addition, I use it to do my homework online.

Grammar

Verb types

Throughout this book there are examples of how to use a range of tenses in your writing and talking. In addition, you need to be able to recognise and identify a range of tenses to show your understanding of reading and listening texts. Make sure you practise the tenses shown here and know how to form the different parts of the verb (conjugate) as well as identify infinitives from conjugated parts.

There are three types of regular verbs in Spanish: those ending with *-ar*, e.g. *comprar* (to buy); those ending with *-er*, e.g. *comer* (to eat); and finally

Hints & tips ⭐

You will find the infinitives in the dictionary so you need to be able to work out the infinitive from the different parts and tenses of verbs.

those ending with *-ir*, e.g. *vivir* (to live). For these verbs in each of the different tenses, you need to remove the infinitive ending (the *-ar*, *-er* or *-ir*) and add endings for the different persons of the verb.

There are also verbs known as 'irregular' verbs because they don't follow the same pattern as regular verbs in the various tenses.

Subject pronouns

The subject pronouns (the words for 'I', 'you', 'he' etc. are not normally used in Spanish as the person of the verb is indicated in the verb ending.

The subject pronouns are:

Key words

yo	I
tú	you (familiar singular)
él	he
ella	she
usted	you (unfamiliar/polite singular)
nosotros / nosotras	we
vosotros / vosotras	you (familiar plural)
ellos	they
ellas	they (feminine)
ustedes	you (unfamiliar/polite plural)

You can, however, use subject pronouns to emphasise or to avoid ambiguity. For example:

Yo soy muy paciente mientras que tú eres muy exigente.	I am very patient whereas you are very demanding.
Roberto y Ana son mis amigos. Él es feliz pero ella es un poco triste.	Roberto and Ana are my friends. He is a happy type of person but she is a little bit sad.

Tenses

Below is a summary of each of the tenses you should know.

Present tense

The present tense is used to refer to what you do or what you are doing.

Regular verbs

The endings for these are as follows:

-ar. *-o* (I), *-as* (you (familiar)), *-a* (he, she, you) *-amos* (we), *-áis* (you (plural familiar)), *-an* (they, you (plural))

-er. *-o, -es, -e, -emos, -éis, -en*

-ir. *-o, -es, -e, -imos, -ís, -en*

Hints & tips

✓ *Make sure you know the irregular verbs off by heart. Regular weekly practice will help you learn them.*

✓ *Use online verb practice sites and write your verbs out to help you learn them.*

For example:

comprar (to buy) → *compro* (I buy)

comer (to eat) → *comemos* (we eat)

vivir (to live) → *viven* (they live)

Stem-changing verbs

In the present tense there are some verbs that change their 'stem' (the part that is left after you remove the infinitive ending). This can happen in all parts of the verb except the 'we' part and the 'you' (familiar, plural) part with verbs such as *pedir* (to ask for) → *pido* (I ask for) and *pensar* (to think) *pienso* → (I think).

Irregular verbs in the present tense

A lot of the irregular verbs in the present tense are common verbs you will use and see every day, such as *ser* (to be) and *tener* (to have). You need to learn these verbs off by heart.

ser: *soy, eres, es, somos, sois, son*

tener: *tengo, tienes, tiene, temenos, tenéis, tienen*

Some others to learn:

estar (to be); **dar** (to give); **hacer** (to do, to make); **ver** (to see); **poner** (to put); **poder** (to be able)

Modal verbs and impersonal expressions

Using modal verbs and impersonal expressions in the present tense can make your language more interesting. For example:

Debo ayudar en casa para ganar un poco de dinero.	I have to help at home in order to earn some money.
Hace falta estudiar mucho para aprobar los exámenes.	You need to study a lot to pass exams.

Perfect tense

This tense translates as what you have done. To form it, use the present tense of *haber* and the past participle of the verb.

haber (to have): *he, has, ha, hemos, habéis, han*

To form the past participle, remove the infinitive ending from the verb and add the following endings:

-ar verbs: *-ado*

-er and *-ir* verbs: *-ido*

For example:

estudiar (to study) → *he estudiado* (I have studied)

beber (to drink) → *has bebido* (you have drunk)

mentir (to lie) → *hemos mentido* (we have lied)

There are some **irregular past participles** that you will need to learn:

hacer (to do, to make) → *hecho* (done, made)
¿Has hecho tus deberes? (Have you done your homework?)

ver (to see) → *visto* (seen)
No he visto esa película. (I haven't seen that film.)

escribir (to write) → *escrito* (written)
Hemos escrito un mensaje electrónico. (We have written an e-mail.)

volver (to return) → *vuelto* (returned)
Mi hermano ha vuelto a casa. (My brother has returned home.)

romper (to break/tear) → *roto* (broken/torn)
Me he roto la pierna. (I've broken my leg.)

You can use the perfect tense in your writing and talking when you are describing things you have or have not done. For example:

Nunca he visitado el sur de España pero me gustaría ir el año que viene.	I have never visited the south of Spain but I would like to go next year.
Mi madre ha decidido que este verano vamos a quedarnos en un hotel en vez de un apartamento.	My mum has decided that this summer we are going to stay in a hotel instead of an apartment.

Preterite tense

The preterite tense describes what you did in the past. To form it, use the following endings after removing the infinitive ending:

-ar verbs: *-é, -aste, -ó, -amos, -asteis, -aron*

-er and -ir verbs: *-í, -iste, -ió, -imos, -isteis, -ieron*

For example:

bailar (to dance) → *Bailé en la discoteca.* (I danced at the disco.)

volver (to return) → *Volvimos a casa después de una semana.* (We returned home after a week.)

Future tenses

To describe what you are going to do or will do in the future, you can use the immediate future ('going to') which is formed with the present tense of the verb *ir + a +* infinitive. For example:

> ### Hints & tips
>
> *If you are talking about how long you have been doing something for and you are still doing it, use the present tense of the verb + 'desde hace' + the time frame. For example: I have studied Spanish for 5 years [and I am continuing to study it]. 'Estudio español desde hace 5 años'.*

> ### Hints & tips
>
> *There are key words in Spanish which signal when you use the preterite tense. For example, when you talk about what you did yesterday ('ayer'), last week ('la semana pasada') or last year ('el año pasado'), these all require you to use the preterite. If you are describing a past holiday, or a past work experience, then use the preterite tense.*

Mañana mis amigos y yo vamos a empezar nuestros exámenes.	Tomorrow my friends and I are going to start our exams
La semana que viene voy a ir de vacaciones con mi mejor amigo.	Next week I'm going to go on holiday with my best friend.

You can also use the simple future tense formed by adding a set of endings to the infinitive of the verb. This is the same set of endings for all types of verbs: *-é, -ás, -á, -emos, -éis, -án*

For example:

ir (to go) → *Iremos a España.* (We will go Spain.)

ver (to watch) → *Esta noche veré una película.* (I will watch a film tonight.)

Some infinitives change:

poder: *podré, podrás* etc.

poner: *pondré, pondrás* etc.

hacer: *haré, harás* etc.

tener: *tendré, tendrás* etc.

Conditional

This is used to talk about what you would do in a situation.

To form it, use the infinitive of the verb and add a set of endings. This is the same set of endings for all types of verbs. This tense also uses the same changes to infinitives as the simple future tense.

Endings: *-ía, -ías, -ía, -íamos, -íais, -ían*

For example:

usar (to use) → *Usaría menos mi móvil.* (I would use my mobile phone less.)

ser (to be) → *Mi trabajo ideal sería en marketing.* (My ideal job would be in marketing.)

Chapter 9

Vocabulary

Throughout your National 5 Spanish course you should be learning and revising vocabulary at least three times a week. This will help you to increase your vocabulary range and also help you to develop further your knowledge of Spanish structures and grammar.

These are the areas covered:

General vocabulary
- numbers, including times, dates, temperatures, distances and prices
- days, months, weeks and years
- weather

Society
- family
- lifestyles
- media
- places in town

Learning
- school subjects
- school – general vocabulary

Employability
- jobs and professions
- work experience

Culture
- planning a trip
- celebrating a special event
- film and television

The vocabulary lists below cover all of these areas. There are also some suggested sentences to show you how to use the vocabulary in sentences for writing (assignment and job e-mail) and talking – presentation and discussion.

Hints & tips

Tips for learning vocabulary

- ✓ *Choose a section of words – focus on about 8–10 words at a time.*
- ✓ *Read them over in English and Spanish.*
- ✓ *Cover up the Spanish words – can you remember how to say them by reading the English equivalent?*
- ✓ *Try the same but the opposite way around – cover up the English and read the Spanish – can you remember what they mean?*
- ✓ *Aim to learn vocabulary at least three times a week.*

General vocabulary

Numbers

uno	one
dos	two
tres	three
cuatro	four
cinco	five
seis	six
siete	seven
ocho	eight
nueve	nine
diez	ten
once	eleven
doce	twelve
trece	thirteen
catorce	fourteen
quince	fifteen
dieciséis	sixteen
diecisiete	seventeen
dieciocho	eighteen
diecinueve	nineteen
veinte	twenty
veintiuno	twenty-one
veintidós	twenty-two
veintitrés	twenty-three
veinticuatro	twenty-four
treinta	thirty
treinta y uno	thirty-one
treinta y dos	thirty-two
cuarenta	forty
cincuenta	fifty
sesenta	sixty
setenta	seventy
ochenta	eighty
noventa	ninety
cien	one hundred
ciento uno	one hundred and one
ciento dos	one hundred and two
doscientos	two hundred
doscientos dos	two hundred and two
trescientos	three hundred

cuatrocientos	four hundred
quinientos	five hundred
seiscientos	six hundred
setecientos	seven hundred
ochocientos	eight hundred
novecientos	nine hundred
mil	one thousand

Time

¿Qué hora es?	What time is it?
Es la una.	It's one o'clock.
y cinco/diez	five/ten past
y cuarto	quarter past
y veinte	twenty past
y veinticinco	twenty-five past
y media	half past
menos veinticinco	twenty-five to
menos veinte	twenty to
menos cuarto	quarter to
menos diez	ten to
menos cinco	five to
Son las dos/tres.	It's two/three o'clock.
Son las doce y cincuenta y dos.	It's 12.52.
la mañana	the morning
la tarde	the afternoon/early evening
la noche	the night
Son las diez de la noche.	It's 10 p.m.
Son las diez de la mañana.	It's 10 a.m.
por la mañana	in the morning
por la tarde	in the afternoon/early evening
por la noche	at night
el amanecer	dawn
el anochecer	dusk
dentro de diez minutos	in 10 minutes time
el mediodía	midday
la medianoche	midnight

Seasons

la primavera	spring
el verano	summer
el otoño	autumn
el invierno	winter

Days

lunes	Monday
martes	Tuesday
miércoles	Wednesday
jueves	Thursday
viernes	Friday
sábado	Saturday
domingo	Sunday

Months

enero	January
febrero	February
marzo	March
abril	April
mayo	May
junio	June
julio	July
agosto	August
septiembre	September
octubre	October
noviembre	November
diciembre	December

Dates and other time phrases

el tres de julio	3 July
el veinte de marzo	20 March
el primero de abril	1 April
jueves, el once de diciembre	Thursday, 11 December
viernes, el veintitrés de abril	Friday, 23 April
Nací el diez de enero.	I was born on 10 January.
hoy	today
mañana	tomorrow
ayer	yesterday
anoche	last night
la semana que viene	next week
el año que viene	next year
el mes	month
el mes pasado	last month
el año pasado	last year
la semana pasada	last week

mil novecientos noventa y nueve	1999
dos mil veintiuno	2021
quince días/dos semanas	a fortnight
siempre	always
nunca	never
de vez en cuando	from time to time
a veces	sometimes
normalmente	normally
raramente	rarely
casi nunca	hardly ever

Weather

Hace mucho frío.	It's freezing.
Está nevando.	It's snowing.
Está nublado.	It's cloudy.
Estamos a 15 grados./ *La temperatura es de 15 grados.*	It's 15 degrees.
Hace (mucho) calor.	It's (very) warm.
Hace (muy) buen tiempo.	It's (very) nice weather.
Hace frío.	It's cold.
Hace mal tiempo.	It's not nice weather.
Hace sol.	It's sunny.
Hace viento.	It's windy.
Hay niebla.	It's foggy.
Hay tormenta.	It's stormy.
Llueve./Está lloviendo.	It's raining.

Society

Family

el/la abuelo/a	grandfather/mother
los abuelos	grandparents
el/la bisabuelo/a	great grandfather/mother
la esposa	wife
el/la gemelo/a	identical twin
el/la hermano/a menor	younger brother/sister
el/la hermanastro/a	step-brother/sister
el/la hermano/a	brother/sister
el/la hermano/a mayor	older brother/sister
el/la hijastro/a	step-son/daughter
el/la hijo/a	son/daughter
la madre	mother
la madrastra	step-mother
el marido	husband
el/la nieto/a	grandson/daughter
el padrastro	step-father
los padres	parents
la pareja; el/la compañero/a	partner
el/la primo/a	cousin
el/la sobrino/a	nephew/niece
el/la tío/a	uncle/uncle
los tíos	uncle and aunt/uncles and aunts

Relationships

Hay una brecha generacional entre mis padres y yo.	There is a generation gap between my parents and me.
Me llevo bien/mal/fenomenal/regular con…	I get on well/badly/really well/OK with…
Mi hermana y yo siempre discutimos por la música.	My sister and I always argue about music.
Mi hermano es mayor que yo.	My brother is older than me.
Mi hermano menor me molesta.	My younger brother annoys me.
Mi primo es menor que mi hermana.	My cousin is younger than my sister.
Mis padres están divorciados.	My parents are divorced.
Mis padres no me entienden.	My parents don't understand me.
No tenemos mucho en común.	We don't have much in common.
No tengo hermanos.	I don't have any brothers or sisters.
Nos llevamos muy bien.	We get on very well with each other.
Podemos hablar de cualquier cosa.	We can talk about anything.

Prefiero compartir mis problemas con mis amigos.	I prefer to share my problems with my friends.
Somos cinco en mi familia.	There are five of us in my family.
Soy hijo único/hija única.	I'm an only child.
Tengo dos hermanos y una hermana.	I have two brothers and a sister.

Home

la casa	house
la cocina	kitchen
el comedor	dining room
el cuarto de baño	bathroom
la habitación	bedroom
el jardín	garden
el piso	flat
el salón	living room

Doing chores

Cocino la comida.	I cook lunch.
Hago el reciclaje.	I do the recycling.
No hago nada en casa.	I don't do anything at home.
Plancho la ropa.	I iron.
Pongo la mesa.	I set the table.
Preparo la cena.	I make dinner.
Quito la mesa.	I clear the table.
Saco el perro a pasear.	I walk the dog.

Town

el banco	bank
la cafetería	cafe
la calle	street
el campo	countryside
el centro comercial	shopping centre
el cine	cinema
la ciudad	large town/city
la clínica	surgery
el colegio	primary school
la costa	coast
la estación de autobuses/trenes	bus/train station
el estadio	stadium
la fábrica	factory
la gasolinera	petrol station
el gran almacén	department store

el hospital	hospital
el hotel	hotel
la iglesia	church
el instituto	high school
la montaña	mountain
la oficina	office
la parada de autobuses	bus stop
la parada de taxis	taxi rank
el parque	park
la piscina	swimming pool
la playa	beach
la plaza	square
la policía	police
el polideportivo	sports centre
el pueblo	village/small town
el puerto	port
el restaurante	restaurant
el supermercado	supermarket
el taller	workshop
la tienda	shop
la universidad	university

Durante las vacaciones mi familia y yo vamos a la costa.	During the holidays my family and I go to the coast.
En mi pueblo hay mucho que hacer.	In my town there is a lot to do.
Hay muchas tiendas de ropa.	There are many clothes shops.
Los fines de semana voy al centro comercial con mis amigos.	At the weekend I go to the shopping centre with my friends.
Mi pueblo no tiene nada.	My town has nothing.
No hay mucho para los jóvenes.	There isn't much for young people.
No hay piscina ni polideportivo.	There isn't a swimming pool or a sports centre.

Leisure

el atletismo	athletics
el baloncesto	basketball
el ciclismo	cycling
el fútbol	football
el golf	golf
la natación	swimming
el patinaje	skating
el rugby	rugby

Mis amigos y yo practicamos la natación los viernes por la noche.	My friends and I go swimming on Friday nights.
Juego al golf con mi padre.	I play golf with my father.
Lo que prefiero hacer es ver la tele.	What I prefer to do is watch TV.
Mi deporte preferido es la vela.	My favourite sport is sailing.
Me gusta el tenis.	I like tennis.
Me gusta jugar a las cartas.	I like playing cards.
Me gustan los videojuegos.	I like video games.
No me gusta nada escuchar música.	I don't like listening to music.
Me encanta leer novelas.	I love to read novels.
Juego en un equipo de rugby.	I play in a rugby team.
Soy miembro de un equipo de fútbol.	I'm a member of a football team.
Nos entrenamos los sábados por la mañana.	We train on Saturday mornings.
Me he apuntado a clases de baile.	I've joined a dance class.

Lifestyles

el bienestar	well being
la comida basura	junk food
el ejercicio	exercise
mantenerse en forma	to keep fit
ponerse en forma	to get fit
la salud física/mental	physical/mental health
Intento no comer mucha comida basura.	I try not to eat too much junk food.
Llevo un estilo de vida saludable.	I have a healthy lifestyle.
Llevo una dieta sana.	I have a healthy diet.
Mantengo una vida equilibrada.	I keep a balanced life.
Soy muy deportista.	I'm very sporty.
Suelo ir al gimnasio por lo menos dos veces a la semana.	I usually go the gym at least twice a week.
Tengo un buen equilibrio en mi vida.	I have a good work-life balance.

Media

chatear	to chat (online only)
la contraseña	password
descargar	download
en línea	on line
escribir a máquina	to type
guardar	to save
Internet	internet

mantener el perfil privado	to keep your profile private
el ordenador	computer
página web	web page/web site
la pantalla	screen
perder	to lose
el perfil	profile
el portátil	laptop
las redes sociales	social media
el Smartphone	Smartphone
subir	upload
el teléfono (móvil)	mobile (phone)

Learning

School subjects

la biología	biology
el español	Spanish
la física	physics
la geografía	geography
la historia	history
el inglés	English
las mates	maths
la política	modern studies
la química	chemistry

En mi instituto tenemos que llevar uniforme.	In my school we have to wear uniform.
Estudio mates/inglés/geografía.	I study maths/English/geography.
Los profesores/profes son simpáticos.	The teachers are nice.
Mi asignatura preferida es la informática.	My favourite subject is computing.
Mi profesor de religión explica muy bien.	My RE teacher explains things very well.
No como chicle en clase.	I don't eat chewing gum in class.
No está permitido correr en los pasillos.	You're not allowed to run in the corridors.
No se me da bien el francés.	I'm not good at French.
Nos ayudan mucho.	They help us a lot.
Se me da bien el dibujo.	I'm good at art and design.
Se me dan fenomenal las mates.	I'm great at maths.
Siempre entrego los deberes a tiempo.	I always hand my homework in on time.

Useful adjectives

aburrido/a	boring
difícil	difficult
fácil	easy
fenomenal	great
informativo/a	informative
interesante	interesting
práctico/a	practical
regular	OK
útil	useful

School – general vocabulary

el/la alumno/a	pupil
aprobar	to pass
la biblioteca	library
la cafetería	cafe/canteen
el campo de fútbol	football pitch
el colegio	primary school
la escuela primaria/secundaria	primary/secondary school
el estadio	stadium
la guardería	nursery
la hora de comer	lunch time
el instituto	high school
pasar un examen	to pass an exam
el patio	courtyard/playground
la pista de baloncesto	basketball court
el/la profesor(a)	teacher
el recreo	break time/interval
suspender	to fail

El año que viene voy a estudiar en la universidad.	Next year I'm going to study at university.
Este año he elegido estudiar inglés e idiomas.	This year I've chosen to study English and languages.
Mi profesor de teatro me da demasiados deberes.	My drama teacher gives me too much homework.
No entiendo muy bien lo que dice mi profesora de matemáticas.	I don't understand very well what my maths teacher says.
Estudio segundo de bachillerato.	I'm doing my Highers.

Employability

Jobs/professions/careers

el/la abogado/a	lawyer/solicitor
el actor/la actriz	actor/actress
el/la albañil	bricklayer
el/la arquitecto/a	architect
el/la asistente de vuelo	flight attendant
buscar trabajo	to look for work
el/la cajero/a	cashier
el/la camarero/a	waiter
el/la cocinero/a	cook
el/la conductor(a) de autobús/taxi	bus/taxi driver
el contrato	contract
el/la dentista	dentist
el/la dependiente	shop/sales assistant
el/la enfermero/a	nurse
estar en paro	to be unemployed
el/la fontanero/a	plumber
el/la ingeniero/a	engineer
el/la jardinero/a	gardener
el/la médico/a	doctor
la oferta de empleo	job offer
el/la periodista	journalist
el/la pintor(a)	painter
el/la policía	police
el/la profesor(a)	teacher
el/la psicólogo/a	psychologist
el/la psiquiatra	psychiatrist
el/la recepcionista	receptionist
el/la secretario/a	secretary

En el futuro voy a ser dentista.	In the future I'm going to be a dentist.
Me gustaría hacerme cocinero.	I would like to become a cook.
Mi madre es médica.	My mother is a doctor.

Work experience

la entrevista	interview
mis prácticas laborales	my work experience
Trabajé en...	I worked in...
una clínica.	a surgery.
un garaje.	a garage.
una oficina.	an office.
una tienda.	a shop.
Tuve que...	I had...
contestar el teléfono.	to answer the telephone.
escribir mensajes electrónicos.	to write e-mails.
hablar con clientes.	to speak to customers.
hacer llamadas.	to make calls.
preparar el café.	to make the coffee.
tomar apuntes.	to take notes.

Aprendí mucho sobre el mundo laboral.	I learned a lot about the world of work.
Empecé a las nueve de la mañana y no terminé hasta las cinco.	I started at nine in the morning and I didn't finish until 5 p.m.
Hice mis prácticas laborales en una fábrica de ropa.	I did my work experience in a clothes factory.
Me llevé muy bien con mis compañeros de trabajo.	I got on very well with my work colleagues.

Culture

Planning a trip

el alojamiento	accommodation
alojarse en un hotel	to stay in a hotel
la arena	sand
bañarse en el mar	to swim in the sea
el camping	campsite
comprar recuerdos	to buy souvenirs
descansar	to rest
la excursión	trip
explorar el mundo	to explore the world
el helado	ice cream
el hotel de cinco estrellas	five-star hotel
ir al extranjero	to go abroad
irse de vacaciones	to go on holiday
el mapa	map
nadar en la piscina	to swim in the pool
la oficina de turismo	tourist office
el piso	apartment
el plano del pueblo	town plan
los platos tradicionales	traditional dishes
relajarse	to relax
la tienda (de campaña)	tent
tomar el sol/broncearse	to sunbathe
visitar otros países	to visit other countries

Travel

a pie	on foot
aeropuerto	the airport
aterrizar	to land
coger un vuelo	to catch a flight
despegar	to take off
en autobús/autocar/avión/barco/ bicicleta/coche/motocicleta/taxi/tren	by bus/coach/plane/boat/ bike/car/motorbike/taxi/train
viajar	to travel

Celebrating a special event

el Año Nuevo	New Year
celebrar	to celebrate
dar un regalo	to give a present
divertirse	to enjoy yourself
el festivo nacional	bank holiday
la fiesta	party
el/la invitado/a	guest
la Navidad	Christmas
la Nochebuena	Christmas Eve
la Nochevieja	New Year's Eve
pasarlo bien/fenomenal	to have a good/great time
los pasatiempos	hobbies/pastimes
el pastel de cumpleaños	birthday cake
recibir un regalo	to receive a present
el regalo	present
soplar las velas	to blow out the candles
el tiempo libre	free time

Film and television

el actor/la actriz	actor
el anuncio	advert
la cadena	channel
la comedia	comedy
los efectos especiales	special effects
la entrada	ticket
entretener	to entertain
entretenido/a	entertaining
informativo/a	informative
los medios de comunicación	the media
las noticias	the news
las palomitas	popcorn
la película de aventuras/ciencia-ficción/ horror	adventure/science-fiction/ horror film
el perrito caliente	hotdog
ponerse al día	to catch up
el programa de realidad	reality show
el pronóstico (del tiempo)	the weather
la serie policiaca	police series
el sonido	sound
transmitir	to stream
ver la tele(visión)	to watch TV
ver programas en línea	to watch programmes online

Space for extra vocabulary and notes on my answer in the writing